BAD ADVICE

Life Coaching from a Blithering Idiot

JACKSON HOLIDAY

BAD ADVICE

Copyright © 2012, by Jackson Holiday.
Cover Copyright © 2012 by Lawrence von Knorr.

NOTE: This is a work of fiction. Names, characters, places and incidents are the product of the author's imagination or are used fictitiously, and any resemblance to actual persons, living or dead, business establishments, events or locales is entirely coincidental.

All rights reserved, including the right to reproduce this book or portions thereof in any form whatsoever. For information contact Sunbury Press, Inc., Subsidiary Rights Dept., 50-A West Main St., Mechanicsburg, PA 17055 USA or legal@sunburypress.com.

For information about special discounts for bulk purchases, please contact Sunbury Press, Inc. Wholesale Dept. at (717) 254-7274 or orders@sunburypress.com.

To request one of our authors for speaking engagements or book signings, please contact Sunbury Press, Inc. Publicity Dept. at publicity@sunburypress.com.

FIRST SUNBURY PRESS EDITION
Printed in the United States of America
September 2012

Trade Paperback ISBN-13: 978-1-62006-105-3
Mobipocket format (Kindle) ISBN: 978-1-62006-106-0
ePub format (Nook) ISBN: 978-1-62006-107-7

Published by:
Sunbury Press
Mechanicsburg, PA
www.sunburypress.com

Mechanicsburg, Pennsylvania USA

Dedication

For Douglas Adams who once said:

The quality of any advice anybody has to offer has to be judged against the quality of life they actually lead.

Thanks for the inspiration ... and the challenge.

Prologue

Shortly after the release of my first book, Who Shit in My Zen Garden? Random Stuff That Spoils My Day, I began getting letters. Several, understandably, were from emotionally wounded Starbucks employees. But most were from ordinary humans seeking advice on everything from home improvement to spiritual well-being.

This frightened me...mostly because I have no talent, experience, or credentials. Seriously, I'm a socially awkward smartass with the people skills of Attila the Hun. Learning to function in the world from me is like learning to ice skate from an accordion. I was upfront about these facts in my initial responses, but the emails kept coming. Go figure.

Now, in the last book, I established that I was a bit of a lazy, greedy dick monkey. And so, rather than write each of you individually, I thought I'd jot all this "wisdom" down in one place and make a little coin in the process. Sure, it's an obvious capitalist response, but what are you, a communist or something?

Anyway, as far as sequels go, I'm hoping it's closer to The Godfather II than Caddyshack II. The latter sucked balls, and I've never had a taste for gobstoppers. So enjoy the guidance. And remember, I'm only trying to help.

Basic Life Skills
*****

"Poor drunks do not find love, Arthur. Poor drunks have very few teeth, they urinate outdoors, and they freeze to death in summer. I can't bear to think of you that way."
— Sir John Gielgud as Hobson in *Arthur*

*****

I've always been an idiot, but I'm strangely comfortable with this reality. A friend once said, "Jackson, you must be really good at your job because you suck at everything else."

Given the correspondence I've received recently, I'm relieved to discover that I'm not the only one who fits into this category. On the whole, I believe people are amazingly stupid. They are also fat, lazy and rhythmically challenged, but that is another matter.

If you ask me (which you did), I think Superman set the bar a little high with his Clark Kent commentary on humanity. Sure, his alter ego is a dork, but he has solid morals to complement the great hair, strong teeth and snappy shoes. This is a lot more than I can say for the primordial soup that spawned the collection of curious cretins that culminated in the cast of *Jersey Shore*. Okay, they have the teeth thing going for them, but I doubt the whole gang possesses the intellectual horsepower to jumpstart a weed whacker. The following questions illustrate a similar trend of uselessness.

JACKSON HOLIDAY

People tell me I have bad breath. Any home remedies?

First of all, stop playing switch. (Sticking one thumb up your ass and the other in your mouth and then, well, switching.) That's no cure for boredom.

Telling someone they have bad breath is one of the most socially awkward things a person can do. The fact that you have multiple people pointing out that your exhalations are corroding your incisors likely means they are on to something.

Normally, I'd advise you to gargle a little propane-and-Clorox cocktail, but I doubt that would squeak by my editor. Corporate lawyers can be pretty touchy. Instead, how about giving the old toothbrush a whirl? Also, the friendly folks at J&J have this new invention called Dental Floss. It does wonders. Of course, if that doesn't do the trick, try crawling under a rock. Oh yeah, and never exhale again.

I'm looking to stand out in formal social settings. Should I wear a bow tie?

Sure, if you want to enhance your overall shmuckiness. There is no upside to bow ties. You either look like a quirky political candidate from the 1940s or a dateless douche at the junior prom, one Star Trek reference away from being stuffed in a locker. Unless you are in a wedding party or defusing a nuclear device in a Bond film, bypass the bow. It just screams, "Trying too hard!" Plus, they're a pain in the ass to tie, and no one likes a clip-on. You can spot those things at night from fifty yards out, and they just multiply the overall loser factor.

BAD ADVICE

I have poor penmanship, but does it really matter anymore?

This is a tough one, only because my handwriting looks like a pack of frightened chickens were set loose in an ink factory. But this isn't about me; I'm happy to shun society. You might have people who you are somewhat fond of and would like to correspond with on an intermittent if not regular basis.

If your cursive is confusing and your print perplexing, take some friggin' calligraphy classes. If you're poor (and that kind of sucks for you), then just run down to the local Catholic school and ask Sister Sledge to work you over with a yardstick. That should give you some motivation.

Letter writing is one of the more tragic casualties of the digital age. In the era of email and iPads, most people struggle with writing their name on a check. You can either stand against the fray or continue to have the visual representation of your literary endeavors make as much sense as the ramblings of a drunken Mexican in Japanese class.

My car is knocking. What can I do? (Sent from an iPhone)

Try turning off the engine, genius. Oh and never text me again. How did you get this number? Only family and age-inappropriate waitresses contact me that way. Family to my chagrin.

JACKSON HOLIDAY

Um, sorry Jackson, but now my car isn't staying still when I get out. (Sent from the same tard monkey)

Are you drunk? Put the brake on, and then throw it in first. Now go lie down in traffic, would ya? Wait, on second thought, if you're the hostess hottie from the Ruth's Chris, come on up. Door's open.

I'm thirty-five. Is it still okay to laugh at fart jokes?

Yes. Farts are funny. I took a night class recently, mostly so I could make snarky comments and hit on co-eds. One evening this chubby dude let one loose. It was like 6.0 on the "ripter" scale of flatulence, and no one laughed... not even a chuckle. Can you believe that? I almost peed my pants, and they just sat there refusing to smile.

Revel in your immaturity, sir. It proves you haven't sold out just yet.

I just inherited my grandfather's tool collection. What's the best way to sell it?

Why, you ungrateful little bastard! How could you sell something, the man spent a lifetime acquiring and truly treasured? Ebaying the collection is just asking for a karmic kick in the balls. Man up, Susan. If you need the extra cash, try getting a side gig, perhaps using the very tools you are about to spin off at below wholesale to some tard monkey in Toluca Lake.

- **A Related Note:** It seems like these days no one can fix anything any more. Broken? No worries. Just throw it away and buy a new one. Some say it's progress, a sign of our technological and financial independence, but it seems to me that the only thing humanity has truly acquired is a deeper sense of futility. We can't fix our cars, our kids, our marriages or our families. It's really rather sad. Perhaps we shouldn't have ditched shop class to go to the mall after all.

My life blows. Sometimes I long to disappear and start over. Should I?

It sounds like you are looking for escape, not a restart button. But sure, if you've got the balls, go. Quit the job. Sell the house. Change your name and your hair color and the way you take your tea. Then settle in somewhere else as someone else. Just know before you cut your ties that you still have to wake up and work and eat dinner and, damn it, you like the way you used to take your tea.

Happiness, my friend, isn't a place or a job or a collection of cohorts. Happiness is something more—something few people ever really understand. So stop being a self-absorbed pecker head and start chasing the right things for the right reasons. Who knows? Maybe you'll find it. Maybe you already have.

I really want to be a writer, but there are so many talented people out there. Should I try anyway?

Listen closely. No, come closer ... closer. That's it, within striking distance of this brick. Let me tell you something about talent. It's like margarine ... a bullshit add-on with almost no value, nutritional or otherwise. We all have some

talent, but it's not nearly as important as you think. In my humble but accurate opinion, talent is:
- A gift, usually as abused as a sixteen-year-old's Lexus.
- A curse. It makes you do things you don't always enjoy, but do anyway because it's loaded with obligation and expectations, some of which is self-imposed.
- Nothing in the face of desire, drive and the willingness to give up everything to get where you want to be.

Talent will always be the bitch of hard work. It's an illusion. I'll have no part of its restrictions and neither should you.

I heard you should open a good bottle of wine first and then sneak in the cheap stuff later. Does that work?

I'm not sure with whom you're drinking, but I only indulge with people I like. Let me give it to you straight, econo-tard: in the company of friends, never be stingy with your heart, time or resources. The outlay is worth the rewards you'll reap. Plus, no one likes a sneaky bastard.

That said, while life is too short to drink bad wine or bed ugly women...if you must, drink first.

Why do people freak out when there is a snowstorm?

In case you haven't noticed, humanity is high-strung. Most people are an email away from going apes hit and taking out a busload of nuns with a nuclear device. The thought of a weather-related "event" that will prevent them from making it to

BAD ADVICE

Starbucks for a morning latte is simply too much to bear.

Personally, I never got the point. Sure, as a lactard I stand firmly against hoarding milk. But people stock up on the craziest, most inconsequential shit. First of all, the world isn't going to end. Plows come, snow melts and guess what soccer moms, you can actually use the four-wheel-drive feature in your military-strength SUV for something other than shuttling your fat offspring to and from their play dates.

Take it from me. If you really feel compelled to exercise your Darwinian tendencies and stock the nest lest you succumb to the more adaptable WASPs in the cul-de-sac, at least play to the theme and gather items that align with an isolated, cabin-like existence. I stockpile porn, beer and beef jerky. Of course, the jerky lasts longer than the beer and the starlets' dreams of parlaying their pole-swallowing talent into a mainstream acting gig, but who needs stale brew or old hoes?

Damn bugs are destroying my garden. I don't want to use pesticide. Any ideas?

What is this, the Home Depot? I bought a house a few years ago and promptly rented it once I realized the homeowner's association wouldn't let me install Astroturf. Gardens are for rednecks and Italians. Well, at least Italians who realize that yelling "*cazzo di merda*" or "*tua mamma bocchinara,*" which loosely translate to "you dickfaced piece of shit" and "your mom's a fluffer," respectively, have no effect on one's agricultural prowess.

Cheer up. Things can always be worse. A friend of mine from Montreal had a similar problem with snails. Apparently, the sneaky little suckers would eat his tomato plants every night and then retreat to wherever the hell snails go during the day.

Hearing the man's tale of woe at dinner one evening, his six-year-old daughter decided to stay up late and take care of the situation herself.

The next morning when the man rose for breakfast he noticed three empty wine bottles in the trash. He interrogated his wife and teenage son and then out of desperation called his baby girl from her room to see if she had any information.

"I got them drunk, Pop," said the industrious tot.

"Why?"

"Wine makes you sleepy. I thought if they were sleeping you could catch 'em."

The father, caught between rage and hysterics, asked, "Well, if you saw them, why didn't you pick them up?"

The kid looked at him as if he were a simpleton and said, "'Cause snails are gross, Dad."

And so the man went to work with the painful knowledge that his daughter was clueless, his alarm system wasn't worth two shits and somewhere in his backyard a collection of drunken Canadian snails were enjoying the hell out of tomatoes that would in all likelihood never become spaghetti sauce.

Count your blessings and head to the supermarket. You'll eat faster and stay saner. I guarantee it.

- **A Related Note:** In case you were wondering, yes, it's a true story. The wine bottles had twist-off caps. Even a Guido kindergartner would have difficulty wielding a corkscrew.

How can I be more creative?

A few months ago, after reading my first book, an old flame contacted me through Facebook. Apparently, my pen name preserves anonymity about as well as tequila shots preserve virginity.

Anyway, after yakking about her second divorce, third kid and fourth round of life coaching with some motivational guru I "really must contact," she invited me to dinner. Normally I'd have opted out, seeing as how people aren't my favorite sport, but I remembered her to be quite gifted in both the culinary and sexual arts. So half a hard-on and a couple of stomach growls later, I was headed to upstate New York.

When I arrived, she kissed me, poured me a glass of wine, and led me to the kitchen, where she was a preparing a pot roast. Not the gourmet meal I'd envisioned, but she was shapely and the wine was smooth. She sorted the ingredients, seasoned the meat and then, to my surprise, cut the ends off the roast and placed it in the oven.

"What's with slicing off the ends?" I asked.

She looked at me as if I had just stepped from a spacecraft. "That's the way it's done."

"Um ... no," I said, pushing the point. "I'm no Iron Chief, but the ends keep the juices in place and actually often turn out to be the best part of the roast."

"That's ridiculous," she retorted. "I've been cooking this for twenty years. I know how it's done."

"But why?"

My challenge flustered her and after a few false starts at a counter argument, she fell silent. Still determined to win, however, she called her mother in hopes of validation. When she answered, my friend confidently clicked on the speaker.

"Hi, Mom. I'm here with Jackson and we're having a little debate about my cooking. You know how we always cut the ends off the roast? He thinks that's the wrong way...."

Her mother's laugh sliced through the remainder of the explanation. "Honey, I cut the ends off the roast when you were a kid because the pan we had was too small."

My friend blushed, offered her mom a soft goodbye and then slugged back a glass of red. "Not a word, Jackson. Not a friggin' word."

The point, people, is that creativity often comes not from learning something new, but from questioning and sometimes letting go of something old. Challenge your beliefs, look at things from different angles and, for God's sake, try not to screw the pooch on the pot roasts of life.

But seriously ...

We all have our talents, some more than others, to be sure. But despite what you've been given, it takes a lot of work to get through the day-to-day grind of living. Still, I have to believe that, while life is harder than you think, it's often better than you expect. You just have to figure out where you stand on the big stuff. The rest will fall into place.

In the end, success is shaped by chance and choices. Knowing which you rely upon can make the whole ride go smoother.

Douchebag Avoidance
*****

"Punch in the Face. For temporary relief of minor douchebaggery, try Punch in the Face today."
— Jackson Holiday, a funny, handsome bastard

*****

The pompous, me-based culture that came to life in the 1980s has only expanded in the subsequent decades. Sure, Gen-Y can tout an interest in saving the planet and attaining work-life balance but only when they are not trying to get on a reality show or invent the next Internet-based time suck. No, I'm afraid that the self-absorbed douchebag culture is only expanding, much like the Borg, only with less leather and more technology.

Someone has to stand against the Skynet-like infiltration of random ass-bag-ness that threatens the very existence of class, culture and social grace. That's not me, of course. I still have trouble using the salad fork. I am, however, willing to make snarky comments until the next wave of apathetic righteousness shows up.

Kurt, you left us too soon.

Jackson, I'm thinking of getting a personalized license plate. Any ideas?

Yes, stick your head in the oven. This sort of state-sponsored Twinkie-dickness makes me want to cause a twenty-car pile-up. The other day I saw this Ford Focus-driving jacktard with a

BAD ADVICE

license plate that read "IBCROZIN." I'm sure he meant to say "IB a delusional dickweed," but someone who drives a Smart Car probably took that.

- **A Related Question: Should I buy a Smart Car?** Yes, of course. After all, it is very smart. You just figured out how to never get laid again.

A friend always says he's "living the dream." He's a loser. How can I point that out without hurting his feelings?

You had me until you mentioned *feelings*. I'm not quite familiar with the term. Still, kudos for taking a stance. I hate that saying, and the over-optimistic assholes who consistently belch it forth.

Just point out the obvious. Say something like, "Dude, I'm glad you're happy, but the trailer park and the new four-wheeler does not a dream make." Then get some new friends. Otherwise I'll have to write a blurb about you, and no good can come from that.

My buddy had the audacity to say that golf was a tougher sport than baseball. How do I convince him otherwise?

Um, you don't. Baseball isn't a sport. It's a game. Anything you can do while chewing tobacco isn't an athletic event. It's kind of like bowling, in that beer and cholesterol-filled foods are actually part of the pastime.

I was going to say that golf was slightly gayer due to the wardrobe factor and players' propensity to hire young boys to carry around their ball bags, but that too is a toss-up. Ball players dress like gang-related mailmen and employ "bat boys" whom they keep confined to a Buffalo Bill-style hole in the ground. Plus, baseball is the only team-based activity that actually has a beer/food break (i.e., the seventh inning stretch) built in. The need for the time-out is ludicrous, given the already slow pace and the fact that most players spend over half the game resting in a sun-shielding alcove.

But don't despair. Lots of activities fall into the "game" category. Track and field, curling, that boring-ass thing old people play on cruises. Oh yeah, shuffleboard. Fishing also belongs in this category, as it's really just an excuse for rednecks to get away from their wives and down a twelve pack.

To be a sport, one must go mano e mano with another athlete and risk physical harm: e.g., boxing, MMA and football. I'll even let basketball, rugby and soccer slide. Those dudes can throw you a whopping, especially in the wrong neighborhood.

Hot yoga can get in as a spectator sport, assuming the practitioners are actually hot. I can so see myself getting hurt going mano e *hot chicko* with one of those broads. But hey, no pain no gain.

- **A Related Note:** Europeans, stop trying to make the case that rugby is tougher than football. I'm not saying that your players are pussies, but I am asserting, correctly so, that football requires a much higher level of badassness. Rugby is a contact sport. Fair enough. But football is an *impact* sport. Sure, they wear helmets and padding, but that's because getting drilled

while airbound from your blind side by two 350-pound linebackers is like being at the ass end of a monster truck traffic accident when you're commuting via Vespa. Walking away from a ten-car pile-up with the willingness to do it again requires significantly more balls than rucking about the pitch trying to score a try...in between all that ass-sniffing, of course.
- **A Second, Somewhat Reluctant Note:** Cricket, though no one fully understands how the hell it's played, is considerably tougher than baseball. I've seen those sports science shows and, while the players wear pads and it may be easier to hit, baseball pitchers don't purposely throw rocks at your shins. That said, both are games, and games are for bitches.

A friend just got promoted and I'm really jealous. This is crazy 'cause I'm actually happy in my job. What can I do?

Congratulate him, and then shut the hell up.

People, men especially, are conditioned to climb some imaginary ladder. Stop being a Penis Erector Set and realize that it is okay to be content. Life is not a human race, *mi amigo*. Plateaus are dandy and often surprisingly short-lived. So enjoy them while they last. Yes, peace of mind may be the only goal worth reaching. If you're blessed with it, rejoice. Don't be fooled into thinking you're missing something; you're probably not.

JACKSON HOLIDAY

I hate telemarketers. How can I get rid of them? Hanging up doesn't do the trick.

These people get rejected hundreds of times per day. A simple insult and a snap of the cell phone won't deter them. To ensure they voluntarily remove you from their call lists, you really have to screw with their psyche. I cut off their sales pitch immediately and dive into one of my own for a useful, yet embarrassing product. Try reading them this little gem next time they mindlessly click through their phone pitch.

Excuse me, but ...
Are you rectorally challenged?
Does your bottom look like the dark and lumpy side of the moon?
Well, you're not alone!!!
Millions of people across America suffer from pesky external ass polyps and unsightly hemorrhoids.
But suffer no more.
With our amazing new "Ass Be Smooth" cream, you will have the confidence to once again proudly display your rectum.
But remember, Ass Be Smooth is not sold in stores. But through the power of intensely aggravating reverse phone marketing, we can offer not 1 but 1.3 bottles of our amazing cream for only 14 billion dollars.
And if you act now, you will receive our amazing "Boog Be Gone" nose-cleaning system absolutely free.
To order send cash or cash to:
69 "Go make time with a monkey" Drive
Piss Off, Maryland, 60060

BAD ADVICE

Or if you'd rather, leave your contact information after our exciting jingle and one of our customer service representatives will contact you at the most inconvenient of times.

(It's important to sing this next part.)
"Ass Be Smooth"
"Ass Be Smooth"
Wanna buy some?
Well...do ya, punk?

Try it, with your best announcer's voice. It works. I haven't had a telemarketing call in about three years.

My friend just got his MBA and now it's all he talks about. How can I get him to chill?

Let me see if I get the picture. Since graduation day, the self-impressed dickweed has been shamelessly attaching the lettering to every available space like some academic dingleberry. Nothing is safe: email signatures, letterhead, even license plates are now embellished with the achievement, even though he went to an online program and graduated class of Thursday.

Don't sweat it. In my experience, the best defense is a good freakin' offense. Start breaking his balls by sending emails with all your kindergarten and Boy Scout achievements. Use as many letters as possible. Unless he is a complete moron, he'll soon realize that one's life should not be sponsored in part by *Sesame Street*.

- **An Afterthought**: Then again, your buddy might not get the subtlety of the statement, since paying for a college education in today's world is about as financially prudent as investing in papier-mâché condoms. Better to be safe. Next time he mentions his scholastic wherewithal, kick him in the dick.

Jackson, have you ever done anything douchey?

Now that, sir, is an excellent question. Of course, I can be the douche master, but the trick is that most of the time I'm completely aware of my actions, which makes them less douchey and more like overt dickery (See the Starbucks douche vs. dick reference in the last book if you are confused).

Still, there are occasions when I unintentionally "Summer's Eve" something. This morning, for example, while singing in the car sans radio, I absentmindedly reached for the dial hoping to "turn that jam up!" I was either really on key or really delusional.

My friend has no game. Any advice?

Sure, "your friend." What are you, in junior high? Man up, we know it's you. This is the douchebag chapter after all. Do you think you're here by accident?

So you're as hip as a rotary cell phone. So you recently joined the Hair Club for Men just to meet people. So your mom just de-friended you on Facebook. Don't be so hard on yourself. I'm sure you have lots of game...Dungeons and Dragons, for example. So freak out not, you know how the ladies love the elf lord... What! What!

Really, just be your nerdy self, and own that shit. Buy a staff, don a robe, and then try hooking up with bitches that get moist at the

BAD ADVICE

mere mention of your personal brand of dork-inspired crazy. Chicks love confidence. Legitimacy of that confidence doesn't seem to matter much. So chin up. Chest out. And Dudley Do-Right your gameless ass into some booty.

How can you get a disturbingly exuberant fan to lighten up without seeming like a bitch?

Well, let me ask you: are you indeed a little bitch? Look, man, I hate the face painters as much as the next guy, but they have the home field advantage, so to speak. Still, there are things you can do. You just have to research the moment.

A few years back, I was watching a Yankee's game in an NYC bar. This cop was standing a few feet from me, screaming at one of the players for his lack of work ethic. When I noticed he wasn't drinking, I asked, "Are you on duty? 'Cause you know, pot/kettle."

The room laughed, and he settled down. Of course I got a parking ticket later for some obscure infraction, but the silence was well worth the fee.

You are always complaining. What makes you smile?

So I'm walking to the coffee shop this morning (think diner, not Star-tards) and as is my habit, I'm working some ideas around and singing to myself. In this case the tune was Billy Joel's "She's Right on Time". Maybe it was the unseasonably cool air. Who knows?

Anyway, as I pass this homeless guy he asks, "Shouldn't *I* be the one talking to myself?"

I stopped, laughed and handed him a twenty. Best money I spent all week.

Is there an easy way to become "mayor" of a location online?

I remember the good old days when people only checked into hotels and mental institutions. Congratulations, you went outside. Now resist the temptation to plug back into the Matrix, you freak. Besides, what are you expecting, a flood of people to zone in on your location and come swarming over to the comic book store to see you? News flash! No one cool gives a shit where you are. The only people who would heed your satellite-sponsored, geographic shout-out are those you should avoid in the first place.

Put down the cell phone and pick up a beer... or dumbbell. Jesus, it's questions like this that make me wonder why I didn't follow my bliss and go into contract killing.

You are always dissing Facebook. Do you have an account and do you do anything douchy like play Farmville?

Yes, I have one and used it to keep in touch with family while overseas. While useful in that regard, I go completely apeshit every time someone posts a prayer, a motivational quote, or a plea for some form of social activism.

Once, in a rather poorly thought out moment of frustrated dickery, I blasted the following update: *"Never repost anything. Have your own thoughts, you mindless biotches. Repost if you agree. Oh crap, I mean... Screw it. Never mind."*

BAD ADVICE

I'm stuck at the airport and this dude is taking three chairs to sleep. The place is packed. Can I wake him and demand a seat?

While I admire the self-righteous rage, I notice you are writing from LaGuardia in New York. You know the saying "never wake a sleeping baby"? Yeah, well, that goes for crazy-ass travelers as well.

Anyone so tired that they muster the wherewithal to snake their body through three impossibly designed chairs in order to sneak in a couple of zzzzs is no one to trifle with. Unless you want to get shanked in the lung with a plastic Sbarro's fork, I'd let the man lie.

What is a hipster?

It's a poorly dressed, liberal-leaning, self-indulgent lun-i-ac that has yet to realize that their androgynous fashion statements have already been run through by Diane Keaton and Elvis Costello. They often attempt to convince themselves of their own coolness by shunning the thoughts, styles and interests of anyone who doesn't freebase lattes while listening incessantly to obscure indie rock. See *douchebag*.

But seriously ...

I understand the optimistic view that all men are created equal. The trouble is, that's just not the case. Some are blessed with robust physical features, while others are ordained with considerable intellectual prowess. Of course, those of us who get the shit end of the stick on both fronts are forced to adapt in order to survive.

But that's not such a bad thing. After all, in a pinch, technique can best the brute. Cleaver can outclass the academic. It's all in the application of one's gifts. The thing is, regardless of what you've been given and what you accumulate along the way, it's best to remain true to the person you are at your core. The easiest way to arrive in chapter de' douche is to fake it. For nothing is more deceitful than false humility.

BAD ADVICE

Dating and Romance
*****

"If I knew anything about love, I would be out there making it, instead of sitting in here talking to you guys."
— Christian Slater as Mark Hunter in *Pump Up the Volume*

*****

Take it from a gameless beta male: success in

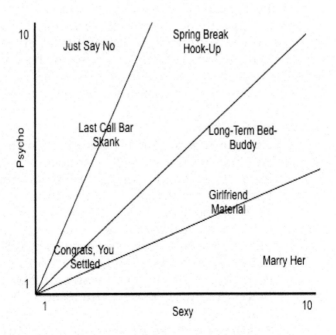

JACKSON HOLIDAY

The following might help expedite your understanding.

- **Sexy**: This most typically refers to a banging body and other wonderful slut-like features, such as come-hither eyes and DSL (dick-sucking lips). Luckily, each man has his own interpretation of sexy. This, of course, isn't a reflection of reality so much as a delusion perpetrated by God in an effort to continue to keep the planet populated. After all, someone has to bang big bitches.
- **Psycho**: Depending on the level, this can refer to anything from mild OCD to full on bat-shit-crazy complete with severed heads in the freezer. Unless you've used a fake name and have a quick exit-strategy (a la out-of-town strange) or an ability to enter the witness protection program in the case of a local booty-based encounter, never exceed an eight on the psycho spectrum. It's just not worth it.
- **Helpful Tips**
  - **Psycho always increases over time.** Bitches never unveil their full crazy level at the beginning of a relationship. Like regular humans, they're initially on their best behavior. Don't fall for this. Stay with a high-scoring crazy chick for more than a week and you'll likely wake up next to Lorena Bobbit. (Google the name if it doesn't ring a bell. One must respect the lessons of history.)
  - **Sexiness always decreases over time.** Even my Jessicas (Biel, Alba and

Simpson) will eventually lose their luster. So start as high on the food chain as you possibly can. Remember, today's size two is likely tomorrow's size ten.

And so, as my chart clearly indicates, there are girls you aspire to wed (if you must marry), those you date and those you hook up with while in a drunken stupor, hoping all the while that your friends never find out. Of course, thanks to Gen-Y's technological advances, your "take one for the team" interlude with the orca-fat East German shot putter will likely go viral.

Regardless of what you're after, motivation gurus often stress the importance of visualizing your goals. For best results, keep a copy of my curve on hand at all times. If I knew anything about marketing, I'd make Jackson's Curve condoms so you can remind yourself what you're getting into...before you, ah, get into it.

As to your more specific romantic woes, I offer the following advice.

What's the most effective love language?

I'm assuming you don't speak Hooker. In that case, I'd opt for Spanish with Chinese subtitles. Forget the pop psychology, Susan. Love is a numbers game. You want to score, you have to shoot the puck. Just be yourself and slap it in there. In my experience, the fun ones like wearing helmets and kneepads, so just go with the theme.

How long should I sleep with twenty-year-old girls?

As long as you possibly can.

Seriously, when asked for the location of the fountain of youth, Kirk Douglas replied, "Easy, it's the saliva of young girls." Sure that's a little creepy, but it doesn't make it wrong.

You seem to do well with the ladies, Jackson. Ever strike out?

My batting average is nine. Seriously, Chaz Bono was a dude for like thirty-seven seconds, and "he" already had better luck with women than I do. I score thanks to unwavering persistence, an inflated ego and the charity of marginally attractive women.

I'm always nervous before a date, especially about my appearance. Is that normal?

A little booger anxiety is okay, but don't obsess. Comb your hair, check the cave for bats, and grab a breath mint. Anything more than that reeks of desperation, and desperate people never get laid.

This works for women, too. I once saw a girl perform the most elaborate pre-date, rear-view-mirror self-check in the history of Starbucks-sponsored courtship. It even came with an AC blow dry/pit check combo. The thing is, she was beautiful. Ah, low self-esteem ... giving beta males a chance in hell.

I just got out of a long marriage and reentered the dating pool. Do I have to worry about VD?

"VD." Really, grandpa? What is this, the 'Nam? No, don't worry. I'm sure you can just march twenty clicks to the *Mash* unit and have

BAD ADVICE

Hawkeye Pierce load you up with some penicillin. That new drug is a miracle worker.

Seriously, brother, there are things out there now that will rot your dick off at the root. My advice is to double-bag it. Bitches be crazy. But I'm sure your mind is a bit clouded from all the weed, so I'll whip up a little musical number to help you recall the PSA. (Just imagine a blues riff and a bit of harmonica. You hippies like that.)

First Verse
Let me tell you about a girl I know.
I did her once and then I did her twice more.
She was so good I went back again.
But when I did, let me tell you, friends ...

Chorus
I caught the clap.
Yeah, I caught the clap.
I caught the clap so bad. The worst I ever had.
I caught the clap.

Second Verse
So let me tell you what I had to do.
I went and saw Dr. Balls B. Blue.
He grabbed a needle 'round two feet long.
I took one look and I was gone.

Repeat Chorus

Third Verse
Well now I'm chillin' out in the sky.
Yup, I'm dead, but let me warn you wise.
The next time a lady wants to play.
Check the chooch and make sure it's okay.

JACKSON HOLIDAY

Repeat Chorus

What's the perfect woman?
For me, it all comes down to balance. I look for high intoxication and low self-esteem.

The girl I'm dating won't commit. What can I do?
That's sweet, Nicky. How's the softball team working out for you? Oh wait. You're a guy. Please turn in your balls and dude membership card at the front desk. The question is null and void.

My boyfriend and I used to talk all the time. Now if the TV isn't on the place is silent. What can I do?
First, thanks for the picture. You're smokin' hot. Sadly, however, that isn't enough once the thrill of the chase subsides. There are plenty of beautiful women out there that someone is tired of screwing. The truth is that sometimes when people run out of things to say it's simply because they stopped doing things worth talking about.

So here's an idea. Track down a snarky writer and give him a world-class blowjob. That's a conversation starter.

Do you think Disney is setting too high a standard for men?
Wait a minute. You read my stuff *and* watch Disney films? I think the marketing guys on Madison Avenue just had an embolism.

I'm going to resist the temptation to crush your soul and give you a straight answer to what is actually an insightful question. Disney is

BAD ADVICE

clearly a female propaganda machine, my friend. Years ago, the WASPy blonde and brunette clique ruled the Imaginary Kingdom. Now you have an expanded force of culturally diverse, kick-ass hotties from Pocahontas and Jasmine to Mulan and Tiana. They even give props to that fish chick Arial.

I have nothing against this, but I ask you, where is Prince Sarcastic? I'll tell you: nowhere. While the women have gotten hotter and more self-assured, the guys are being portrayed as bumbling idiots who would be lost with out their estrogen-filled counterparts. Where is our character development?

I say they start letting realistic guys wind up with the princesses. And no, Shrek is not realistic. Maybe if they lower the bar just a little I'd have a shot with Belle, the hottest hottie in cartoon land.

- A Related Note: I dig Belle cause of those big brown eyes and overall classiness. Plus, she was willing to date a beast, which gave me hope of someday finding love. Of course, a friend recently crushed my optimism by pointing out that he was in fact a bazillionare and, well, probably hung like a beast. Bastard!

My boyfriend is really nice and looks great on paper, but there's something missing. He asked me to marry him. What should I say?

"Goodbye". Believe me, there is a big difference between saying, "I love you" and "I love you, but..." The latter never ends well. Save yourself the heartache and the lawyer fees. Oh, and stop with the "looks good on paper" shit. That just screams "gold digger".

JACKSON HOLIDAY

I finally landed a hot chick and now I'm jealous all the time. What should I do?

Drink.

Seriously, that's the trouble with dating beautiful women: there's always someone waiting in the wings to talk her right out of your arms. Granted, she's probably a self-indulgent ho-bag, but it's not all her fault. Things change. You'll get bored, notice her quirks, even grow tired of her specific brand of monkey lovin'. The excuse doesn't matter. The "other guy" hunts the wounded, and chances are you're going to inflict an emotional bruise or two. A flock will surround her sooner than you think. You'll look up and she'll be gone, living a life that at least part of you will want back.

So yeah, order another and make it a double.

I'm scared to ask this, but do you believe in soul mates?

These days I barely believe in soul food. But that's more about timing than anything else. For example, I met an interesting girl recently, a real brain with great legs. We had a nice conversation, but my Spidey sense said it wouldn't stick. It's not her fault. I'm just broken.

So yeah, I'm a believer, but only 'cause I've seen one up close and missed the boat. That's the trouble with finding your soul mate so early in life — if you screw it up you're sentenced to a lifetime of almosts, second bests and near misses.

I suspect a lot of people go home every night to their second-string lover. Some are okay with it, but not me. Sometimes I think the biggest pricks are disenfranchised romantics. My advice

BAD ADVICE

is to keep believing. Just be quiet about it lest some jaded bastard breaks your balls.

Could you fall in love without ever seeing the girl?

While *The Lake House* and *Sleepless in Seattle* are romantic concepts, you usually can't get a feel for crazy until it's staring you in the face. I'm all for love letters once you're actually in love, but I like to meet first. Plus, I have the penmanship of a drunken lama and a typed love letter is as romantic as a colonoscopy.

What are your thoughts on beer goggles?

You can hammer a nail with a screwdriver, but it's not ideal. Sure, you'll get the picture on the wall, but it's likely to sit crooked and leave a crack that, while no one else can see it, you know is there.

But hey, sometimes you just need to get laid, so drink up. Just know that she'll be a whole lot less interesting once the Wolf* wears off.

- ***Holy crap, it's a friggin' footnote:** According to the Oxford Bottled Beer database, Wolf: *Granny Wouldn't Like It* is a dark reddish-brown brew that sports a malty aroma, a persistent smokiness and a hint of chocolate. I never tried the English ale, but as a fan of alliteration I really needed a beer starting with W to end that last sentence. Ah, the Brits. You can always count on them in a pinch.

I heard you spent some time in Asia. Are the girls easy?

Easy? Yes. Desirable? Well that's where the complications set in.

During the tail end of a recent trip to Phuket, Thailand, I busied myself with some last-minute shopping. You know, haggling my way into a few knock-off t-shirts that were over-priced at sixteen cents. Yeah, you don't get good deals in Asia. At best, you get slightly less screwed than the buyer before you.

Anyway, just as I secured a "morning price" for a "top quality" Bobby Bahamas shirt, these two rather attractive girls zipped by on a scooter. Having seen me, they pulled a U-turn, navigated their ancient shit-cycle through the littered and rain-soaked street and began cat-calling with the proficiency of a New Jersey construction worker.

Accustomed to such melodic shenanigans, I simply smiled, waved them off and stole a passing glance at their overall hotness. It was the last bit that haunts my dreams. Sensing my interest, they spun around for a second pass, with the driver again sing-songing her desires and elaborate pricing matrix. When I again refused, the passenger who had been silent until this point, threw up her hands and, in what I would imagine was the best Wolfman Jack impersonation this side of the mainland, asked, "So what, you don't want sex?"

There is beauty and ease all over the world. Just be mindful that, like everything else, if sex comes too easy, it comes with a price.

How important is it to date a girl with money?

Depends. Are you poor?

BAD ADVICE

No one wants a broke bitch, but in my heart of hearts I really don't care about money. I care about purpose. Find someone who lives within her means and above her yesterdays and you've found someone to hold on to.

Oh, and what's with the gold digger-ness? In my experience, what looks bad on a woman looks worse on a man. Get a job and grow a pair, not necessarily in that order.

How do you know that you've found the one?

Listen, Neo, I'm not sure if you are talking in terms of the Matrix, the Highlander, or some other quasi-metaphysical nonsense, so you really need to clarify this shit. I'm dispensing advice, not fortune cookies. But let's assume you mean a chick, or, in your case, a Brad-o-licous life partner.

Everyone has a list. The shit you want, your deal breakers, the stuff in the middle you're willing to put up with, but only if she is really hot and not a big slut bag like your ex. The thing is, when you meet the one, you completely forget you ever drafted the list. It doesn't apply. She names the cat. You kiss the girl. And you don't give a shit that you just made reference to a Hepburn movie. If you're eating breakfast with an angel, what grief can anyone give you?

I'm not having any luck with the ladies on Match.com. Any advice?

This one could take a while.

1. Lower Your Standards

Lots of guys logon to dating sites hoping to find a billionaire supermodel nymphomaniac with

JACKSON HOLIDAY

an affinity for beer, sports and lesbian porn. But let's face it. If they did exist, chances are they're not going to go for a forty-five-year-old creepster with a beer gut and a bad comb-over. Don't despair. Love is out there. It's just bigger, older and much less attractive than your initial fantasy. Want to score a Match.com date? Simple. Adjust your "About Her" write-up to a more realistic realm. Oh, I don't know, maybe something like:

"Friends insist that I'm simply too demanding, but finding the ideal woman isn't like picking up a loaf of bread. For me, there really are some things that are true non-negotiables.

Take love for animals. I need a girl with at least fifteen cats...two of which, are ideally named after psychotic ex-boyfriends who drop by occasionally around 3 a.m., you know, just to say hi.

Keen intellect and a sense of adventure are also good qualities so Mafia connections, access to automatic weapons and knowledge of the ins and outs of extradition law are big pluses in my book.

Speaking of work, money management is a vital life skill. If someone can't balance the demands of her bookie, crack dealer and Amway salesperson well enough to maintain a credit score in the high teens, well, I hate to be materialistic, but she's probably not the one for me.

And then there's religion. Sure, some would be okay with an honorable existence and an occasional mass, but they're slackers. I want a girl who knows Jesus well enough to score an autographed Noah jersey.

BAD ADVICE

Of course, we're nothing without our mental well-being, but in this fast-paced world it's hard to achieve bliss on your own. That's why I want a heavily medicated woman who, at the instruction of her court-appointed psychiatrist, is engaged in a variety of group counseling and intervention programs.

Finally, I'm no George Clooney, but I'd be lying if I said I wasn't into beautiful women. There just has to be that initial attraction. That's why I really appreciate blurry glamour shots, pictures of your pet, obscure nature scenes and, of course, those family photos from the Reagan administration.

2. Get musical on the biotches

Women love singers. This is not an opinion. The only reason Lyle Lovett gets laid is because several far-sighted country skanks were ear-fucked into believing that he has charisma. I'm not casting aspersions on the subliminally euphemistic last-name-having six-string picker. We all work with what we have. But really, the man's a laryngitis case away from jerking off to the Sears tool catalog.

Still, there's a lesson to be had. Even if you sound like a cat in a blender (never a bad decision) you can achieve a similar effect through the use of musical poetry. Work this old school jam into your online profile and you'll get more mail than Santa.

Let's Plan Our Escape
I was tired of the club scene,
picking up in the bars.
Reading all about Venus,

JACKSON HOLIDAY

and how they're nothing like Mars.
So I logged on to Match.com
and browsed the headlines in bed,
And under "Drama Free Woman,"
there was this ad that I read:

"If you like pina coladas,
and have never done time.
If you won't sleep with my sister,
and are not total slime.
If you like kissing in the moonlight,
and will call the next day,
I'm the lady you've looked for,
answer me right away."

Well, her picture was gorgeous
and she seemed kinda sweet.
But I'd have to be different
if I were to compete.
So I jazzed up my profile,
(no I've never skied in Peru),
But the rest was real clever,
and quite possibly true.

"Yes, I like pina coladas,
and a have a great job.
My family's Italian,
but no, not the mob.
And I'm not on medication,
there's no baggage to claim.
Send me love in a letter,
and life won't be the same."

So I'm waiting with high hopes
till she gets back to me.

Hope she's cool as I picture
and we fit perfectly.
Then I'm all done with Match
and her bio is new.
It reads "this ad's null and void
cause I found somebody who...

"... likes pina coladas,
and the warm summer rain.
And the sound of the ocean,
and the taste of champagne.
He likes making love anytime,
oh the man should wear a cape.
Yes this ad has expired,
cause we've made our escape."

3. Give them a pre-date questionnaire

Romantic and witty attracts as much crazy as it does everything else. Cut through the nonsense by asking the following in the "About Her" section of your online profile.

- Were you "once a man"?
- Are you on any "special medication"?
- Did you graduate high school (and no, a GED doesn't count)?
- Do you have a job, preferably a career, ideally one you love?
- Do you owe money to the mob?
- Do you talk about Jesus like you're racquetball partners?
- Do you sound like an extra on *The Dukes of Hazard* or *Jersey Shore*?
- Was your picture was taken during this presidential administration?
- Are you a raging alcoholic?

- Are you "finding yourself," "getting in tune with your inner child" or habitually taking dating advice from Doctor (insert random first name here).

I'm not going to tell you what the right answers are, of course. It depends on what you're looking for. But in my experience, this tends to weed the out the lunatics.

- **A Related Note for the Ladies:** Listen up, Match.com girls. Don't post a ten-year-old cover picture of yourself looking hot in a bikini and follow it up with a reality series of you posing awkwardly, marginally covered in a stretched-out pop tent. I'm no meteorologist, but that's just bad advertising.

What's the craziest Match.com headline you've ever seen?

This one chick wrote, "What you see is what you get." And she didn't have a picture. So...many...jokes.

What's the best way to start a Match date?

No clue, but I know the worst.

A few weeks ago, I decided to meet this chick for coffee. She was late, as most women are on first dates, and so I busied myself with some work-related email. When she finally arrived, she appeared disheveled and upset. She apologized and recounted some tale of woe about her kitten's psychological difficulties (lost on me). Then she nervously repeated the apology, noting that she was "just so busy with my career".

BAD ADVICE

She had great legs and so, in an attempt to ease her mind and salvage the chance of booty acquisition, I tried my hand at empathy. "Hey, no worries," I assured her. "My life is pretty busy too, and I sometimes run late. I just didn't realize what I dick I was being."

Silence bitch-slapped the setting, a stunned look pole-vaulted its way to her countenance, and she asked, "Did you just call me a dick?"

We both knew I had, albeit inadvertently, and that kind of spoiled my chances of getting laid for the price of an espresso. Still, to her credit, she laughed it off, and we both scored a story about the guy who called a girl a penis proper within the first thirty seconds of a first date.

Ah, one's literary muse. She's elusive for sure, but you never expect her to popup from behind the coffee counter and kick you in the nuts.

- **A Related Note:** Coffee is the ideal first date, especially when it comes to Internet affairs. First of all, it's cheap. Not that I'm a fan of frugality, but let's face it, people spice up their profiles (and by that I mean lie their asses off). No point in spending big bucks on someone who shows up to the bantamweight weigh-in dressed in full sumo gear. Also, it's quick. No one drinks six cups of coffee. Go for drinks or dinner and you could be stuck there all night. With coffee, you can either order an espresso and be out in a flash or, in the rare case she actually appears as advertised, linger over a latte and then continue at an alternate location... preferably somewhere with condom accompaniment.

JACKSON HOLIDAY

What first-date errors do women make?

Being late. Look, we get it. You don't want to be the one lingering at the bar waiting for some romantically challenged net-tard to come strolling though the door with false hope and hard-on in hand. That's understandable. Just arrive within ten minutes of the appointed hour.

Nothing is worse that sitting awkwardly atop a bar stool trying to convince yourself and the "seen it all before" barman that you're actually interested in the women's field hockey game they're showing on ESPN 9000. The only thing worse is when some politically inclined cocktail monkey has the news on without subtitles, and you are forced to dick around with your smart phone while avoiding glancing at the door every thirty seconds.

Again, we get it. Waiting sucks. But since we're probably going to pick up the check, the least you can do is get your big ass to the Bennigan's on time.

Should you ever disclose "your number"?

Conventional wisdom says no. You should leave history in the past. The thing is, I'm neither orthodox nor intelligent. I always ask. Granted, bitches will lie, but you can discount the standard six to eight response in a second. When pressed, the second answer usually reveals something closer to the truth.

Why is this important? Sure, it's a helpful factoid in the rare case she says something like, "This week? Oh, well, about thirty-seven, but I was sick on Saturday." But mostly it's just a great way to get a baseline on her poker face. Everyone

BAD ADVICE

lies when asked about the number of people they've slept with. Up or down, the nature of the lie doesn't matter. What does matter is that, if you're observant, you can learn her "tell," and that will pay dividends.

- **A Related Note:** One thing both parties need to disclose is dramatic weight loss. Of course we'll be impressed with your ability to shed a hundred pounds of grammar school weight. We'll also sign you up for a gym membership and hide the Twinkies. No point in tempting fate.

What is the least confrontational way to break up with someone? I was thinking email.

Wow, I didn't realize eunuchs could date. Good for you. Seriously, if you don't have the balls to do a face-to-face, you shouldn't be in the game. Kicking someone to the curb via text, tweet, email or Facebook post is just a chicken-shit thing to do. Why not just issue them an "un-e-vite" to the douchebag party that is you?

Phone break-ups are bad enough, but ending a relationship via electronic medium is just plain rude. And that's coming from me. Man up and then sit her down for a heart-to-heart. Karma's a vengeful bitch, so do the right thing lest the next time a girl shit-cans you, it will be via a gay-strip-o-gram at an important work function.

An old acquaintance just got hitched. Why do I miss the girl I never really noticed?

Didn't the Jackson Five cover this issue in 1969 with "I Want You Back"? It was a great song. I could do without the velour pimp hat on a six-year-old, of course, but great song nonetheless.

People are attracted to the unattainable. They long for what is just beyond their grasp. That's no surprise. Falling in love is often a lot more attractive than being in love. So when the door shuts; when the option of that most magical part is taken off the table, it's only natural to get the blues.

It happened to me once. We dated briefly, but I kept it cool. Somehow cool turned to cold and so she sought warmth in the arms of another. I wasn't surprised. Heck, at the time I wasn't even fazed. But there are times when I wonder if I missed an important plot point in my life. As if this girl could have kept me tethered to something substantial, something real.

If you're like me, you'll try to fill the void with friends, hobbies, or a slew of quasi relationships with emotionally unavailable lovers. But in the end, we are left to wrestle with the reality of our isolation, the haunting sting of loneliness our inaction helped create. The scary part is that, since we never asked, we'll never know how the story might have played out.

Sometimes our choices come back to bite us. But at least we have the soundtrack to the memory and that can help soothe the soul.

But seriously ...

I don't know Jack about Jill when it comes to relationships. Heck, I've been good and bad with women, often in the same conversation. I guess that's why this chapter is such an orgy of ideas. Still, one of the first questions I received via the

BAD ADVICE

website (www.whoshitinmyzengarden.com) involved love. It asked if I believed.

Fair enough. I said I would answer anything that didn't involve solving for x. So here goes.

Yes, I believe. In fact, I recommend it. I recommend love knowing full well that whatever and whoever you seek will almost never be whatever and whoever you wind up with. I recommend love knowing that you'll likely get your heart broken repeatedly. I do because there will be days when you look into her eyes and the whole goddamn world will disappear. In that moment, worries recede and you'll have the kind of happiness you can carry around and pull out on the days when the rain never seems to end.

I'm not smoking the pipe. I know the work often outweighs the wows. But for me, the leap is worth the fall. So yeah, having lost two potential soulmates, I continuously keep an eye out for a third and hope that she is somewhere looking for me. I also hope that she has an ass you can bounce a quarter off of, but that's another matter.

Friendship
*****

"Friendship is the only choice in life you can make that's yours! You can't choose your family! Goddamn it, I've had to face that! No man should be judged for whatever direction his dick goes! That's like blaming a compass for pointing north, for Chrissake! Friendship is all we have. We chose each other. How could you fuck it up? How could you make us look so bad?"
— Raul Julia as Carlos in *Tequila Sunrise*

*****

To avoid any confusion on the matter, when I speak of "friends" in this chapter I'm referring to people you actually know, call on occasion and perhaps see socially...you know, for a beer or to take in a ball game. What I'm distinctly *not* referring to are the scores of scantily clad hooker wannabes you've friended on Myspace, or the collection of long-lost grammar school acquaintances you've latched onto through Facebook in hopes of discovering they've grown fatter than you.

These people are not your friends. The slut monkeys accepted you to stroke their own egos. You'll never meet or screw them. As for the kindergarten contingent, they live four states away, are after the same voyeuristic indulgences you are and probably never liked you.

Real friends will drive you to the airport, help you move and lie to the police to keep you out of

BAD ADVICE

the joint. Take stock of those few you can truly trust with the title. The sobering analysis might be depressing at first, but at least you'll know whom you can borrow money from and that's always helpful, especially when it's for bail.

My buddy is a slacker. How can I help him get his act together?

Try a healthy dose of reality. Say something like, "Billy Jo Bob, I just saw you pick up a disemboweled raccoon carcass from the side of the road and stuff it in a plastic hazardous waste sack. Granted, after your shift at the old animal control center you'll head to the local watering hole and bait shop, down a twelve-pack of discount malt liquor and then stumble home to play a little game of unprotected poke in the whiskers with the old lady, thereby degrading the human gene pool even further...but really, there has to be more to life. How about a couple of Tony Robin's tapes and a spin on the elliptical machine?

My friend says I watch too much television. How much is too much?

What is this, a PBS after-school special? If you are emotionally invested in the Real Housewives' romantic entanglements, chances are you need to put down the remote. My buddy had this revelation during a barroom chat that I've since dubbed the "Mousekebeers" episode. Let's drop in on the conversation, which was conveniently taped before a live studio audience...hence the laugh tracks.

"I think I saw a cockamouse!"

JACKSON HOLIDAY

As you might expect, I called the Marshall wannabe an idiot and motioned to the waitress for another round.

"Dude, I'm serious," he said.

"I believe you. I saw one of those things once. It was really depressing."

"Depressing? We're talking about a half-roach-half-mouse, right?"

"Don't be ridiculous," I said. "Those things don't exist."

"But you just said you saw one. What the heck is a cockamouse?"

I paused for dramatic effect, spread my arms wide and said, "It's a mouse with a big cock."

So kids, what did we learn from this? Simple: too much TV can make you shoot beer out of your nose. It can also get you the phone number of an eavesdropping waitress, but let's not spoil the learning.

Should I go into business with my friend?

No. Friends and business go together like herpes and anything else. If the guy is more of an acquaintance, lawyer up and go through the motions as if he were a stranger. If he's a true pal, run. Friends are harder to make than money, especially as you get older. Respect their value and act accordingly.

My friend is in a terrible relationship. He is a smart guy, but he just doesn't see it. What's up with him?

Pussy causes retardation. So does dick, or so I'm told. Being in a relationship that involves hot sex will take a monkey wrench to anyone's common sensibilities.

BAD ADVICE

It reminds me of my flying days. Although I was just after the basics, my instructor wanted to give me a lesson in instrument navigation on the off chance I flew into a cloudbank and lost my way. (Think JFK Jr. and you'll appreciate the wisdom of his suggestion.)

Anyway, he made me wear one of those giant blaster hoods (think Luke Skywalker during light saber training or any ass-crack-sporting wielder you may have come into contact with recently). He then dick-monkeyed with the aircraft, flipping it about and making me long to projectile vomit. Once I achieved the proper state of green, he released the controls and asked me to position the plane back to straight and level flight using only the instruments.

In this situation, much like a relationship, you can't trust your body. Every fiber of your being will insist you are headed upward while every instrument will point out, correctly so, that you are spiraling down toward your doom. Mind your friends when you're in love. They can often see the approaching mountain of heartbreak you can't quite spot through the cloud of bliss. The reality check is a painful piece of co-piloting, but a lot less so than challenging the ground to a punching match.

My Gen-Y colleagues are always going on about how Millennials are better than Gen-Xers. Any ammunition to the contrary?

Sure, Gen-Y has the web and tweeting and phones the size of breath mints, but we have Han Solo, and that dude is still cooler than all the other shit combined. Seriously, what are they going to come back with, Dane Cook? He is about as relevant as Myspace.

- **Related Note:** All generations have their cool points and their debacles, so avoid going head to head with someone who has a brain. Remember, for every Miley Cyrus, there is a Billie Ray.

Friends— how many of us have them?

Fantastic, Whodini. You earn a gold star for that question. Now get your nose out of the nice man's asshole.

Should I loan my friend money?

Unless you're a bank or a loan shark, you don't make loans, you give gifts. If you approach things with that mindset, you'll never be disappointed, and you may end up pleasantly surprised. Can't afford to permanently part with the cash? Don't. Debt between friends is like honey between thighs. It might seem like a good idea, but trust me, it isn't.

I lost a good friend today. Not sure how or why, but he's gone. Any hope of him coming back around?

I'm going to make some assumptions here. First, that when you say "friend" you actually mean a lengthy, platonic, meaningful relationship and not some dude you banged in the back of a pickup in the CVS parking lot. I'll also assume, given your gayed-up signature, that you are one of those artsy literary chicks who might actually off herself if I go overboard with the sarcasm.

So in an attempt at actually helping I'll refer to the much-loved "Reason, Season, Lifetime" poem that's been bouncing about the Internet. You have to decide why he was there in the first place. Did one of you want or need something specific and now that the transaction is complete, he's flown the coop? Or has he been around a while, but just never made it into the forever category? Only you can know for sure.

We've all been through it. For me, it was a girl named Megan. She was married, and we were cheating. There was a physical part, of course, but not right away. It started, as these things often do, with little betrayals of the heart that morph slowly from fondness into full-blown love. She came to her senses eventually. Her husband was great, and I'm nobody's best bet. Still, I have to believe it was about more than just wild monkey lovin'. She was there for a purpose.

Years before, a girl I loved checked out far too soon to digest. I thought I'd be numb forever, but then came Megs and her crazy optimistic outlook. Simply put, she woke me up. She showed me that even in the midst of my deepest despair, my most troubled mind, a woman, the right woman, could touch my heart.

I don't believe in altruism. After all, we both got the thrill of something new. Still, I can't help thinking that she risked everything to teach me this lesson, to get me out of my own way.

Don't despair, artsy chick. Good things will come around. And in the meantime, you can sleep with me. I love a thoughtful babe. They tend to cook and give backrubs.

JACKSON HOLIDAY

My friend asked me to pet sit. Do I have an obligation here?

Been there. My friend Jennifer watched my house while I was on assignment in Singapore. Actually, she just watched over the useless corporate tard monkeys who were supposed to be watching my house. One can never be too careful. Anyway, soon after I returned, she had occasion to be away for a week and asked if I would care for her two dogs. Normally, I'd have refused, but given her recent servitude it was hard to be my usual dickish self.

The two canines in question were Mortimer, a barely mobile hound dog and Moxy, a 750-year-old pug, with asthma, a lazy eye and an affinity for drool. Now she must have been desperate because the Darth Vader-like dog and I were long-standing enemies. Okay, maybe "enemies" is a strong word, but if ever the hacking cylinder of Snausages went missing, the folks down at CSI would peg me as a person of interest for sure.

I arrived on day one of the ordeal and de-crated the hound. After a brief belly rub and an assurance that we'd soon amble about the neighborhood, I went to the dungeon where they kept the creature. I approached cautiously, thought about making a dark-side joke, and instead opted for the high road, hoping to befriend the genetic experiment gone astray.

"Hey Moxy. Looks like we're stuck with each other. So let's make the best of things, okay? How you doing today, buddy?"

The dog, which had never been known for his comic timing, looked up, let out two disturbingly labored breaths, and died on the spot.

"You have got to be shitting me," I said.

BAD ADVICE

As if on cue, the dog relieved itself a final time, expiring in full slapstick style. So there I was, staring at a crate full of crap-covered canine, when it dawned on me that I had approximately zero animal-death-management experience.

My friend was unreachable, the vet unknown and all my Italian quasi-connected compadres were four states away. With no one to turn to, I relied on instinct. I found a small carpet, rolled the beast up and headed for the trunk. Something about this must have seemed wrong to Mother Nature, 'cause as I attempted to hoist the carcass into the car, my sister-in-law called and asked about my day.

Too discombobulated to concoct a believable cover, I confessed my predicament and asked for advice. She, with disconcerting efficiency, came up with a variety of hide-the-body locations and then, after I'd convinced her there was no foul play, secured the location of the nearest vet hospital.

Apparently there is some sort of dead dog procedure at these places, because a kaleidoscope of well-intentioned PETA people attempted to console me. Unfortunately, by this point the shock of the event had worn off and I was already thinking in terms of comedic undertones. Luckily, the animal babes mistook my giggling for a defense mechanism and tried to console me with gentle hands and, later...two phone numbers.

I reached Jen that evening and conveyed, with my best attempt at empathy, a G-rated version of her pup's demise. The bitch of it was that she was only two days into a week-long vacation, which meant I had a workweek full of canine caretaking left. As I drove to the house the next day, I thought of Mortimer and subconsciously chanted a simple prayer. "Please don't be dead. Please don't be dead."

Long and short: unless you are some sort of dog whisperer, skip the sitting. If you are on the ass end of a favor, kick in for a kennel. Trust me it's cheaper and less emotionally draining.

How can I shake an old high school friend? I've moved on.

No you haven't. If you had, you wouldn't be bitching up an e-storm of literary whininess. Seriously, I asked for questions not dissertations, for fuck's sake.

Relationships change, you post-frat-pledge-tard. Too often, people beat themselves up over how they should feel and what they should say because of some attachment held decades before. The feelings might have been genuine years ago, but feelings are fleeting and yours, it seems, have long since lost the letterman jacket.

Don't waste energy lugging around emotional suitcases. You have to pay for the privilege now, and TSA agents are a bunch of ball breakers. You can occasionally travel down Memory Lane if you like, but it's doubtful that the road trip will rekindle something lost or, more likely, never found. That's like playing an old record and thinking it's the same. Sure, it sounds familiar, but the people and places and events that made the rhythm move you are long gone. It's just noise now. Sweet, perhaps, but noise just the same. High school tunes never sound as good as they did on prom night. It's time to get a new song.

BAD ADVICE

My buddy has been really depressed since his girlfriend left him. I don't want to be melodramatic, but he's joked of suicide. Should I be hiding knives?

Much to the dismay of the Nicholas Sparks crowd, relentless faith in the happy-ending scenario isn't everyone's default setting. And despite his press, Santa doesn't quite have the work ethic we were led to believe. Sadly, reality is real.

The question reminds me of an old friend...someone I haven't thought of in years. He was one of those who got short-changed on the optimistic end of the gene pool and as a result, elected to check out of the Earth Hotel prematurely.

It was a bad call, to be sure, the impulsive, emotional kind troubled kids make when they think they are alone. I've always thought suicide to be as senseless as walking out of a World War II film 'cause some extra forgot to remove his digital watch. Yeah, it was a mistake, but missteps are part of the business. In the end, fewer people notice than you imagine. Fewer care.

The thing to remember is that one's life story is little more than a messy first draft, complete with false starts, bad jokes and placeholder lovers. Our friendships end awkwardly in prepositions and more often than not our romantic participles dangle hopelessly, just daring the critics to mock our imperfection. The good news is that our lives are supposed to be drafted in pencil. We're given a setting to be sure. But even if you're religiously inclined, no one really pays attention to the script. You can edit as you go. That's the beauty of improvisation.

You never really know the why of these things, which of course is cause for the ultimate frustration. Maybe he needed an editorial eye, a bit of banter to expand the plot, perhaps a better friend. In any case, I can't help but feel my silence failed him.

If you're serious, don't dick around. Get him to a pro immediately. Being called a wanker for worrying is better than weeping alone any day. Put down the book and make the call.

But seriously ...

Candor is the hallmark of friendship. With every other relationship, be it family, professional or romantic, you have the hazards of obligations, expectations and hierarchical horseshit. The result? Well, you never really know where you stand.

Friends, on the other hand, will give it to you straight. A buddy was fond of saying, "Jackson, you're a real piece of work." I always took it as a compliment. He set me straight one day over beers. Friends do that.

BAD ADVICE

Health and Body Issues
*****

"I'm lookin' for the fountain of middle age."
— Rodney Dangerfield as Thorton Melon in *Back to School*

*****

I never understood why, but people tend to confide in me. It's baffling. I mean, let's think about it for a moment. I'm moody, sarcastic and rarely have a nice word to say. In short, I'm kind of a dick. Still, children approach me with reckless inquiry, babies and old people shuffle in my direction babbling incoherent tales of triumph and woe and normal humans think it perfectly sane to divulge their most intimate encounters, knowing full well that they'll receive three parts bashing for every one part wisdom. Perhaps that's the secret sauce of the interpersonal relationship. One would think you'd need more sugar. Then again, people are fat enough.

Anyway, this buddy of mine started bitching about his various anatomical tribulations. He began by mumbling an obligatory thank you for having his limbs, faculties and a disease-free countenance, and then launched into a list of shit that doesn't quite work. He professed to have more pain-in-the-ass problems than most people – lactose intolerance, dandruff, psoriasis, tinnitus, anxiety disorder, irritable bowel syndrome, low self-esteem and what I'd imagine to be a rather small and stumpy penis. Okay, so I added that last one. What? It's a safe bet.

Anyway, his hissy fit got me thinking. If this Nancy boy can earn a good living and enjoy a reasonable social life despite his physical annoyances, how much could he achieve if they were removed?

I'm not sure if I believe in heaven and perfection and all that, but having your body operate at 100% efficiency as designed would be pretty sweet. Maybe we should organize a strike against a deity to be named later and demand better working conditions. People love a good protest. In the meantime, here's my take on your body-related woes and related inquires.

What is the least I can do and still say I'm a triathlete?

I don't know whether to be disgusted by your laziness or impressed with your sense of honor. I'm sure there is some official rulebook, but I'm not going to read it. Ironman, triathlons – just a bunch of show-offs. Here's what you do. Take a bath, do a lap on a stationary bike and then run an errand. There you go. You're a triathlete.

Can guys pee with a boner?

Yes, my little slut monkey. Of course, in my case I have to jockey around like a crane operator for a few minutes lest I whiz on the bathmat. But it can be done. My drunken, blue-balled self assures you of this.

BAD ADVICE

I heard that sometimes guys don't pee in a straight line. Is that true?

What's up with you and the fascination with pee? If you really want R. Kelly's phone number, just ask.

However, it is a valid question. Yes, sometimes our love faucet can go a little haywire. One morning, after a particularly fun evening of drinking and screwing, I awoke to find my penis working like a busted sprinkler. Thank God for hand towels and Febreze.

Should I try to be a vegetarian?

No, vegetarians suck.

I tried to be a vegetarian once, and after about an hour I found myself rewriting Metallica's song "One":

Veggies imprisoning me.

All that I eat is fresh, crispy produce.

I cannot live on this crap.

Someone give me a burger.

(It sounds better with the guitars. You know, the ones in my mind.)

Ever hear of someone stopping midway through puberty? My voice changed, but I can't grow a mustache. Should I be worried?

Why would you want to grow a mustache? Planning on abducting some children or being in a seventies-style porno? Rejoice, you creepster. You'll save thousands in razors. Plus you'll appreciate the baby face when you get older. The youthful appearance will help you continue to bang college girls well into your thirties. Just make sure they are indeed legal.

JACKSON HOLIDAY

- **A Related Note:** Of course, I could be off about the delayed puberty thing. I knew this one guy who at forty-one finally mustered the biological wherewithal to grow a five o'clock shadow. (It took him four days and all, but let's not trifle about with the details.) That was the good news. The bad news: it came in with the pattern of a graying Joe Dirt. Count your blessings and nail the coeds while you can.

My doctor says I have to take a laxative... Should I?

Not in my store, you don't.

"Hummala bebhuhla zeebuhla boobuhla hummala bebhuhla zeebuhla bop...."

Thank you Mr. Roth. Boom!

What are you thoughts on health food?

I'm against it. I think the liberal media has gone overboard with all this health talk. Real men live on steak, beer and beer-battered steak fries. Yup, in my book, Crisco is considered a legitimate side dish.

You know what the real health risk is? Jogging. Being a headband-toting road-tard is more hazardous to your physical well-being than freebasing an unfiltered Camel while doing lines off a hooker's hip bone. Not only are you more likely to get bounced off the hood of a Buick, but your recently health-conscious ass is also apt to keel over from a cardiac arrest.

People talk about a runner's high, but that's just bullshit. I've seen joggers up close. Most resemble a miserable, asthmatic Darth Vader one kilometer away from a pine box.

BAD ADVICE

- **A Related Note:** Don't push those wonder shakes on me. Be honest. They taste like flatulent donkey ass. You need to build up a tolerance to a variety of cuisine. You can't shun 90% of the food pyramid in favor of some vitamin-infused protein contraption. Do that and risk the reality of croaking the first time you sneak a Snickers bar. Well, at least it will really satisfy my craving for health-tard elimination.

The other day on Dr. Phil...

Stop it. First of all, you're in the wrong chapter. That bald, pudgy shyster is focused on messing with your head, not your body. Though, in fairness, he will mess with your head about the status of your body. And second, don't trust any medical "professional" who doesn't have the energy to consistently mutter his last name.

I'm not saying that Phil is a doctor like Dr. Jay is a doctor. For all I know, he dispenses advice with the crispness of Dr. Pepper, the authority of Dr. Ruth and the poetic fluidity of Dr. Suess. The thing of it is, he's a divorced, post-middle-aged bald guy shouting love advice from a convertible corvette. How reliable can he really be?

Are drugs really that big a deal? All my friends seem into them.

Couple of things here: Let's assume that you know a hundred people, which you don't. Most people know about ten people really well, followed by a slew of acquaintances. But let's give you the benefit of the doubt.

JACKSON HOLIDAY

Would it be fair to say that there are at least a hundred assholes in the world? And if so, that they tend to congregate much like hipsters, Amway salesmen and fans of Coldplay?

Okay, assuming we are aligned in that, I'm afraid that you have simply become an asshole magnet. Everyone is not into drugs — just the desperate dick monkeys with whom you surround yourself. I'm not one to preach, but if Gen-Y was smart enough to champion the anti-smoking craze, then you should have the intellectual wherewithal to realize that it's probably not a good idea to pop a pill scored from some random psycho with a chemistry set.

Yeah, raves might be more fun on E, but that's just because they make you forget you're with a bunch of other flabby fuckers who are far more appealing when you're stoned. Have a drink or nine, fire up a blunt if you must, but do yourself a favor and skip anything that could land you in the ER after one try.

What are your thoughts on medical marijuana?

Given the shit storm of biological woes the average person has to deal with, I couldn't fault anyone for employing a little legal loophole *party of the first part* dickery. That said, if you are firing up a fatty every time you get a hangnail, your claims of medicinal use might be farfetched. My only concern with pot usage is to ensure that no one ever Bogarts a blunt.

How do I get the most out of my **Men's Health** *subscription?*

Put it down and get your ass in the gym.

BAD ADVICE

The health craze has done wonders for making people rethink their lifestyles. And in truth, you can get a lot of helpful tips from such publications. The thing is, knowledge is useless if not applied consistently. My advice is to read it on the elliptical machine. You'll likely learn that the apparatus isn't doing nearly what you hoped. That's okay — since you're already in the gym you can start cross-training and really make a dent in those love handles.

- **A Related Note:** Attention men's magazines. Stop giving advice on supplements. If we actually consumed everything as implied, we'd croak on the spot. I appreciate the thoughts on how to make brussels sprouts taste less like aardvark ass, but we both know I'm going to opt for the bacon burger. Give me a couple more tips on how I can break the ten-rep chin-up barrier. We'll both feel better, and I won't die of vitamin proficiency.

Do I look fat in these jeans, Jackson?

Um...you're not wearing jeans. But thanks for the picture. Look, honey, unless this was taken at the house of mirrors, I'd say you need a sandwich more than an ego boost.

Seriously, what's with people and a lack of self-esteem? Granted, there are a plethora of overconfident chubsters out there who swear they are supermodel hot even though they sport back fat, six chins and a caboose that beeps when they do the moonwalk. Still, I'm less concerned with their psychological health than that of those who squint endlessly into a mirror searching for flaws that aren't there.

I don't know if it's marketing, media or misguided mothers, but something is screwing with the psyche of young American women. I'm no activist, but when a 5'8" high school senior is too embarrassed to don a prom dress because the scale clicked over to triple digits, something is seriously wrong with the world. Again, I'm not one for copulating with the pleasantly plump, but boning a babe that looks like a twelve-year-old boy is just creepy.

- **A Related Note:** Never let an opportunity to do the moonwalk pass you by. MJ may have been a crazy, chimp-loving eccentric, but the man gave us a cool move we could all master. And it looks a helluva lot cooler than the Macarena.

Does masturbation make you gay?

Wow, so how long has the compound had access to the Internet?

Listen, cult boy. There's nothing wrong with a little self-loving. Whether you call it spanking the monkey, choking the chicken, waving the one-eyed wonder wand, or simply jerking off, the rumors surrounding the activity are just that... rumors. You won't go blind, get acne or grow hair on your palms. Depending on the frequency with which you fling your phallus and your inclination to ambidextrously arm-wrestle Henry Longfellow, you may actually develop Popeye-like forearms. And since chicks dig muscles, you could conceivably wank your way out of a single status. So worry not, my pious pud-puller. Assuming you have lotion and a willing, non-roofied tube sock, you should be good to go.

- **Point of Order**: This response assumed that you were in fact beating your own bishop. If you meant to indicate your desire to varnish a pal's pole, well then, yes...you're probably mitten gay with a side order of track lighting and show tunes.

How drunk is too drunk?

We've all experimented with the one that is one too many. Years ago, after being introduced to a trio of fine fellows – Jim, Jack and Johnny – I found myself arguing with a belligerent bloke who had the audacity to insinuate that he was better looking than me. After about twenty minutes (and apparently several pictures), a friend pointed out that I was debating with a mirror.

Luckily, the pictures never surfaced. I credit this in part to timing, as the event happened pre-Facebook. But in fairness, I'd have to attribute my good fortune to mutual blackmail. You see, a few weeks later my pal got so toasted at a backyard BBQ that when he reached for the porch door he missed and careened helplessly into the bushes. Yes, that's right. He was so drunk that he literally missed the whole house. Now *that's* a home movie to remember!

I think a good goal is to strive for the perfect state of inebriation: one where your inhibitions retreat, but your wits remain. I'm sure that's a mythical mirage, but so is Santa and yet we all still look forward to Christmas. Merry, merry.

JACKSON HOLIDAY

Are panic attacks a real thing?

No, they're fake things that seem pretty freakin' real at the time. A friend once described them as that moment when you see a cop's flashing lights in your review mirror. Not so bad, right? Yeah, the trouble is that the cop is a starving lion with a medical degree and he tells you that you're dying of cancer just before biting your face off.

The mind is a pretty powerful and sometimes scary organ. Still, as I understand it, anxiety disorder is a largely controllable condition that can be bested with the right resources. I'm no proctologist, but I'd avoid WebMD, put in a little gym time, and try not to down a bottle of Jack at every meal.

- **A Related Note:** Try not to break people's balls when they mention the affliction. Sure, it might seem like horseshit, but that's what the average person thought about schizophrenia years ago. Better to goof on things like restless leg syndrome. I imagine fewer serial killers have that, plus…you know…it sounds sorta gay.

But seriously …

People often tout the advances in medical science, but frankly, I'm just not impressed. Sure, the statisticians will insist that we are living longer, but at what expense to quality of life? Creaking through the mall on a tricked-out power scooter while tethered to a portable lung, a pacemaker and a chemo IV drip is not a happy existence.

We have the best researchers in the world and yet, despite all the money we've pumped into the

BAD ADVICE

medical community, we haven't cured a fucking thing since polio — and apparently even that is making a comeback. Lose a leg? Screw you, here's a Captain Hook-like piece of pine. Born blind? Can I interest you in a canine companion? Oh, and what's that, a nasty fall severed your spine? No worries, just run...um, okay, perhaps roll...on down to the nearest Ikea and pick up a plush piece of mobile upholstery.

The average citizen is stepping up their game in terms of healthy living. Most of us have stopped smoking, disavowed hard-core drugs and spend more time in the gym than on a bar stool. So how's about a little leadership?

I'm not sure Neil Armstrong ever made it beyond the sound stage, but I think the world is overdue for another moon-shot rallying cry... something akin to a president confidently declaring, "We will, before the next decade is through, cure cancer." Who knows if we'd actually achieve the goal? But one thing is certain: if you don't shoot for the stars, you sit on the ground.

JACKSON HOLIDAY

Office Life
*****

"The thing is, Bob, it's not that I'm lazy, it's that I just don't care."
— Ron Livingston as Peter Gibbons, *Office Space*

*****

I hate unions. Mostly because they've outlived their usefulness. Sure, there was time when companies treated women like power tools and forced six year olds to work fourteen-hour shifts in coal mines for nineteen cents a week, but overt white-collar dickery aside, corporations these days tend to behave themselves. So what was once a productive necessity has morphed into a collection of bureaucratic ass bandits who serve only to reduce worker efficiency, inflate operational costs and bitch-slap our competitive edge.

That said, I think the pendulum is starting to swing to the point where the common man could once again use a little protection. I say this because today there are no barriers...no down time. Sure, in a service-based economy most of us don't have to punch in on the loading dock. The trouble is, we never truly punch out.

At last count, my boss had six media through which to randomly harass me. Texts, email and instant messages coupled with a trifecta of phone lines virtually assure our continuous connection. Add old-fashioned, in-person meetings and we

BAD ADVICE

spend more time together than most married couples.

Perhaps this is simply the reality of operating in a global marketplace. Time is money, and if you want the latter you must be willing to give up the former for the privilege. The thing is, we've never quite shaken the Puritan work ethic. The Europeans will drop off the planet when *on holiday*. The Asians can tai chi their way to emotional well-being. American knowledge workers, on the other hand, are provided a meager two weeks of vacation that they are often afraid to take.

Perhaps the fear is rooted in insecurity. After all, who can afford to pause in the middle of a race? Maybe the tortoise did have a thing or two on the hare when it came to the big picture. Then again, sometimes the best way to stay connected is to unplug. We all have our working woes. Here is my take on yours.

The girl at work is trying to destroy me. How can I get back at her?

Destroy you? Really? According to your letter, you work at the sunglasses kiosk at the mall. Head down to the food court, have a Slurpee, and chill the freak out. Then sign yourself up for a few courses over at the community college. You are light years from having any hierarchy-related work woes, princess.

My boss takes credit for everything I do. Can I call him on it?

Um, no. Stop being a crybaby. Besides, it's probably not as bad as you think. People usually know who is who in the zoo. He'll likely slip up

JACKSON HOLIDAY

and get his due.

When you've done great work and received no credit, remember that there are often some real morons standing on the shoulders of giants. Your turn will come as top person in the chicken fight of corporate life, and I hope you have the courage to give credit to whom it's due when the time comes.

I just got offered my dream job, but it's on the other side of the country. I'm worried that if I turn it down I'll be living in my parents' basement forever. What should I do?

The hardest choices come at the times when you are the least prepared to deal with them. But then again, if life were a breeze the victories would have no meaning. I believe that people are exactly where they most want to be. Where do you see yourself? If it's not where you are, get packing.

I'm a terrible negotiator. Any tips I can use?

I got your tips right here, my friend. (And yes, I was holding my penis when I said that.) Here are my top ten negotiating tips.

1. **The Power of Intimidation:** People are basically wimps who can be easily taken advantage of. Bark, threaten and push them around to get what you want.
2. **Inflate Your Value:** You're probably worth less than you think, but that doesn't mean you have to settle. Exaggerate your experience and/or sales numbers to get more for yourself.
3. **Harass People into Submission:** Badgering works. People get tired of saying

no, so ask them a million times until they cave.

4. **Blackmail:** Sure it's illegal, but it's almost impossible to prove in the corporate sector. Find out what your boss or counterpart does wrong, photograph it and then sell them out.
5. **Be Emotional:** No one likes a bore. Quiet people are weak, and the weak get crushed in negotiations. Laugh sporadically throughout the day for no apparent reason. And yell! People really respect yelling...it makes it easier to listen.
6. **Mark Your Territory**: No, don't whip your dick out and pee on the carpet, but make sure people know exactly with whom they are dealing. Whenever possible, stand up during meetings, even if you are not the one speaking. Also, if the situation presents itself, beat your chest and talk in an aggressive tone.
7. **Discover and Expose Your Counterpart's Weaknesses:** If your counterpart doesn't know something, make damn sure that everyone else finds out. This will make them appear stupid and weak, and they will likely cave to your demands.
8. **Never Concede Anything:** In negotiations there are winners and there are losers. You can't win everything, but by being an immobile, belligerent bastard you can be certain you'll never make a concession. Better the both of you get nothing. Win-win is for pussies.
9. **Manage Nay-Sayers and Know-it-alls:** Nay-sayers are gutless homos. Bullying

tactics work well with these people. Also, overload them with work in the hopes they will quit or die of an untimely heart attack. Know-it-alls are just as bad. Make them appear stupid in public. That will teach them.

10. **Never Underestimate the Use of Force:** The only downside to using violence is the risk of jail time. But what are you anyway, a wuss? If you don't have the stomach for it, hire someone. That's why they make Italians.

I have a business idea, but I'm scared to make the leap from my job. Should I go for it?

Help me out here. Your letter says you work as the night manager of a Circle K gas station. What exactly would you be giving up?

Let me tell you a little story about the kind of karmic ass-kicking procrastination can dish out. In January of 1996, I came up with a business idea to put people's CVs online and tie recruiters and job hunters together. The company was called (don't laugh, jerk-wad) Resumania.

Yeah, yeah. I know it's showtune gay, but I actually had a product, unlike those IPO-having, cash-grabbing, corporate dick monkeys over at LinkedIn. Now, I had no connections, technical savvy or financial wherewithal to make it happen. Heck, I'm writing this thing on a stone tablet. But in truth, I probably could have given it a go. Don't punk out on your ideas. You'll regret it.

BAD ADVICE

Are there any non-verbal mistakes you can make in an interview?

Well, I suggest your don't pick your nose, scratch your balls or flick the hiring manager the bird. Aside from that, I think the shrink industry is really making too much of all this nonsense. Yes, sometimes I cross my arms when I think you're an asshole. And okay, perhaps I'm unconsciously shielding myself from your stupidity. But you know, sometimes I'm just friggin' cold.

Years ago, back when I tried to be a productive member of society, I met with a corporate recruiter. After sort of hitting on me (which was creepy 'cause at the time she seemed all crusty old...like forty) she started in on how my overall presence was standing in the way of my leadership potential.

"Jackson," she said, "let's start with your self-expression. You shouldn't put your hand to your face when you talk. It says that you're hiding something and are closed off emotionally."

While this was before emoticons and annoying text-inspired acronyms, I somehow managed to shoot her a "WTF" look. Of course, when Miss Pop Psychologist missed the plot, I followed up with the actual words.

"Really?" I added, sensing the job and sexual exploit slipping away. "Did you ever think that maybe I was just hiding a zit or that my chin actually itched? I mean seriously, I doubt scratching one's facial features is a sign of some deep-rooted psychological problem, and it certainly doesn't have anything to do with job performance."

JACKSON HOLIDAY

She swallowed nervously and fidgeted with the underside of her desk. "Um, true, but you *could* smile more."

I flashed a look that was distinctly not a smile. "Sure, it's nice to post a grin every once in a while, but should I really be going for the gay game-show-host look? Anyone can spot a phony smile. You're doing it now. It doesn't make you approachable. It makes you look like a serial killer."

Well, at that point she stood up, tentatively offered her hand and punched the security button she'd been searching for (apparently all nonverbal cues for "get this crazy bastard out of my office").

As I was leaving (ah, being escorted out), I yelled, "You really should work on that handshake of yours. Unconsciously, it says you're a self-aggrandizing douche-monkey."

Yeah, I didn't work for a while. But it was worth it.

I think I'm giving too much to work and I feel out of balance. What can I do?

A buddy of mine worked on a recent presidential campaign. The good news is that after two years of eighteen-hour days and sacrificing everything for the cause, his guy won. The bad news is that he had an emotional breakdown as he tried to convey the soul-crushing sense of disappointment he felt when he learned that the person he believed in was not only unable to keep his promises, but never really intended to do so. He said it was akin to discovering there's no Santa or to realizing your first love won't be your last. This very tough man

BAD ADVICE

cried right there in my living room, an action that while understandable, is still something I break his chops about.

We all have an internal compass. When things are in harmony, it points north and we progress on work, family and personal goals. However, when you have an electrical shit storm of crazy that unnaturally pulls the needle, you'll get lost. There's no escaping that Magellan-sponsored reality.

Mind your compass and watch the weather. That's the only advice I can give.

I'm afraid I won't succeed. Is there anything worse than being a failure? I'm terrified, seriously.

Failure is bad. I'm not one to sugar-coat things. But standing still is the only way to ensure that outcome. Don't forfeit your life, you little bitch. Strap on your helmet and set your mind to body-checking fate into the boards.

Get it? Good. Now suit up and hit the ice. Just remember as you do that failure isn't the only thing you have to worry about. A far worse fate is to succeed in the wrong direction. Let that bounce about the ice for a while.

My manager just shot me a blue screen of death. Is my career over?

I'm a bit lost, since I like girls and use a Mac, but I'll go on the assumption that you're employing a nerd-like reference to indicate you recently had a bad performance review.

Put those analytical skills to use, my friend. If this is a one-off, either learn from the feedback if you deem it valuable or toss it aside. If the guy is a powerful player or you have a boatload of corroborating data that points to a trend, you might want to place stock in the opinion and get your ass in gear.

Regardless, I wouldn't sweat it too much. The world will always need geeks. It's not like you have a liberal arts degree and need to perpetually pucker up to an ass cheek to ensure your survival. Best case, it's a glitch in the Matrix. Worst case, you'll have to reboot your career. That's why I do all my writing on an Etch A Sketch. There's something comforting about being a shake or two away from a fresh start.

Can I over-use the IM feature at work?

Yes. Yes, you can. IMing is like sneezing in someone's face without saying "Excuse me." I'd shy away from that techno-doucheness, especially if you're a Gen-Y person. We already don't take you seriously. And, whether you know it or not, you're one emoticon away from being shit-canned.

If you *must* IM me, do so sparingly and get to the friggin' point. Don't start with "Hi. How are you?" I understand that you're being friendly, but in essence you are trying to build rapport using a tool designed specifically to eliminate rapport-building. Stop it.

Oh yeah, and on the off chance that we are actually friends, try not to start your messages by calling me a dick or making reference to the admin you banged in the break room. Those are bar stories. They usually don't go over so well when I'm making a presentation to the board of directors.

BAD ADVICE

Do those free webinars have any value?

No. If something is free it either sucks gorilla cock or it comes with fine print. In this case, the small font indicates that they now have your contact info and will ruthlessly badger you to buy the stuff they actually sell. Nothing is free, baby. Count on it.

This is petty, but why elevator music?

This is simply a prank the workingmen played on the office folk. A classic blue-collar/white-collar power struggle where the nerds lose and the kings of gym class reign once again.

Unless you are rocking a three-minute elevator excursion, any sort of musical interlude is pointless. If you like the tune, you're out before its conclusion. More often, of course, you hear just enough to have some gayed up version of a Stone's song sheared into your skull.

Some will say the mind-numbing sounds of Muzak soothes unsettled nerves so the claustrophobia-inclined don't go apeshit and kill everyone else in the box; but I say it's class warfare, plain and simple. Of course, I tend to overthink things.

I'm so sick of marketing. It's everywhere. Why?

'Cause it works. Forget bottled water. Think "essential" oils. There is a whole industry devoted to selling women various forms of scented Crisco for fifty bucks an ounce. What's so essential about a lavender mist air rejuvenator? Are you shitting me? People are sheep.

Don't fight it. Use the concept to your advantage. If essential oils can break the billion-dollar mark, someone will fall for the concept of "vital blowjobs."

Are people getting dumber? I look at my work colleagues and fear for the safety of the planet.

A friend and his coworkers were recently relocated to another building. In an effort to be helpful, one of the administrative staff posted everyone's new contact information and job titles in the common area.

My buddy's abbreviated title was "Cyber" (it's a government thing not a porn thing) and he, trying to be funny, penciled in "Ninja" after it. Two months later he received an email from the group's admin requesting he proofread his business card. It said, and I shit you not, "Cyber Ninja Specialist."

Yes, people are getting dumber.

How can you tell when you've really bonded with your employees?

First, never use the word "bonded" in the workplace again. I'm not sure, but with all the political correctness these days I think that would be grounds for a sexual-harassment lawsuit.

Oh, wait. It just occurred to me that you may have meant "befriending" as opposed to "bending over the conference table". My mistake. But come on, *bonding* is close to *bondage* after all, so cut me some slack.

For me, it's all about the little things. The following IM exchange illustrates the point at which you just catch someone's drift.

Employee: It's Friday. YAY!

Jackson: Did you just all caps me a yay?

BAD ADVICE

Employee: You could use a yay or two. Happy weekend!!
Jackson: Yes, it appears we made it.
Employee: ...through the rain...
Jackson: You just sang that part out loud, didn't you?
Employee: Hehehehe, busted.
- **A Related Note:** The person I was conversing with was in Singapore, which is twelve hours ahead. This would explain both my use of the IM feature and her apparent intoxication.

But seriously ...

For many people the work/life balance thing is a misstep away from falling off the highwire of life. And judging from the last two economic meltdowns, despite our efforts most of us are performing without a net. In many ways, I'm no different.

I'm not sure when exactly the title changed hands, but I awoke recently to discover that my soul was not my own. It happened slowly. No mystical crossroads in the Deep South. No contract-wielding Lucifer swindling away my signature with a blood-spewing Mont Blanc. There was no big moment of truth, and there certainly was no tangible upside. And that's perhaps the saddest part. I didn't broker my essence for life-altering fame, fortune and the company of age-inappropriate women. I let it go for contentment; the emotional, financial and social equivalent of a Sunday afternoon spent in a recliner.

There are upsides to my lifestyle. I don't do anything any more. A kaleidoscope of day players enter my life for an hour or so, their walk-on roles ensuring that the lawn gets mowed, the oil gets changed and the house that never quite felt like home maintains its museum-like ambiance. It was an investment, after all, and you never know when it will be time to sell.

Scratch that. I think it's time. There's something I need to buy back, and the cash will come in handy.

BAD ADVICE

Travel and World Affairs
*****

"Hey look kids, there's Big Ben, and there's Parliament."
– Chevy Chase as Clark Griswold, *European Vacation*

*****

Crowds make me nervous. Any time a mass of people think something is a great idea, my Spidey sense goes ape shit. Why? 'Cause people are stupid. Sure, get to know them individually and you might find a few here and there that you don't want to strangle. But together they are a collection of emotionally unstable, bloodthirsty zealots, a riot away from becoming placard-carrying cannibals.

Religious gatherings, government institutions, Amway rallies...no good comes from mass quantities of humans emphatically chanting the same force-fed ideology. Most individuals start off stupid. You simply increase the inefficiency, multiply the bureaucracy and quadruple the crazy with each new member.

The problem worsens when you add the complexity of cultural nuance. That's why it best to avoid foreigners all together. That's just crazy with an accent. Of course the hippies will have you believe that global harmony is but a *We Are the World* remake away. The truth, however, is a bit more complex.

JACKSON HOLIDAY

No matter what I do, I'll never understand what it was like to go to high school in Shanghai. That's the bitch of culture. It's not something you can see on a tourist visa. You have to swallow the red pill to see the Matrix. My advice is to skip culture and groups and tackle people one at a time. At least then you have a fighting chance at understanding. Here's some more related wisdom.

I'm seventeen. Next year I can go to war, but I can't buy a beer. What's up with that?

It's bullshit. However...while "kids" often advocate a lower drinking age, I think we should leave the law alone and instead raise the age that our children are allowed to fight and die. I think eighty-seven is a fine figure. Can you envision a war with all eighty-seven-year-olds? There'd be a huge argument about the price of milk in 1927 and then a nap.

I just saw a hybrid-only parking space at trendy new restaurant. Is that for real?

No, that's someone's political agenda, and I don't put up with it. I've seen them and consistently park my Camaro in those spots, smiling through the looks of disdain as I do.

First of all, that is not a law. Handicap parking is a law and should be respected. I'd even be okay with "Retired Veteran" parking 'cause we owe those folks more than we can ever repay. But hybrid parking? That's just stupid. Even if it was a law, it doesn't make any sense.

Congratulations, tree-hugger, you just forced me to circle the block nine times in my three-gallons-to-the-mile Hummer. Way to save the planet.

BAD ADVICE

Have we gone too far with political correctness? I feel like I have to watch everything I say.

We jumped that shark long ago, my friend. I've completely abandoned political correctness in favor of this new concept called honesty. It's great. I act like me and invite others to do the same. It can be dicey at first if you are used to being a psychological servant of the mainstream social agenda, but it often produces surprising results.

A while back I stopped at a convenience store to pick up some condoms. (Okay, fine, it was a 40-ounce and a *Hustler*.) Anyway, being a friendly fellow, I greeted the cashier.

"What's up, Habeeb?"

The guy got all flustered, put down his Koran and said, "My name is not Habeeb. Do I look like a Habeeb to you?"

"Yes. Yes you do."

He thought for a moment, smiled and said, "Fair enough. But my name is Leonard."

"Really?"

"No. But it could be, you bastard. You shouldn't assume. It's very rude."

"So what is it?" I asked, extending my hand.

"Kareem."

"You're shitting me?"

He smiled again and said, "I am shitting you not, you Ken-doll-looking mother-fucker."

We've been friends for about six months now.

I want to save the world. Any ideas?

You're shitting me? Listen, Tinker Bell, I realize that you're a liberal and as such you have

JACKSON HOLIDAY

the unrealistic liberal-like tendencies. That's not all bad. Heck, I donate to the Little Rat Bastard...um...I mean, Children International. The thing is, the world doesn't need saving. In fact, I talked to the world just the other day. It's says it's fine — pretty peachy, actually...a little smog over LA and Beijing, but otherwise okay.

What? Oh, right. The world just called you an asshole.

I'm doing the European backpacking thing after high school. Any travel advice?

Yeah, stay home. Europeans hate us, and the chicks, while no longer furry, have long since realized that guys are guys, and they all lie for sex no matter where they come from. Plus, Euro-hoes think Americans are douchebags, and that never helps one's game. If you *must* travel, my advice is to head to Asia. They still hate us, but the women are easy and the food is cheap.

Despite your destination, just remember two things: you get what you pay for on the accommodation front, and shampoo is friggin' heavy. (Actually there is a third thing, the most important for any traveler. Mind your towel. RIP Mr. Adams.)

Whatever happened to American Indians?

They've been busy running casinos and negotiating subsidies for never-to-be-built nuclear-waste facilities. There are a few still around, of course, but they're kinda pissed about us stealing their land and slaughtering their people.

I learned this the hard way recently, and so I offer this brief cultural PSA. If you find yourself

BAD ADVICE

with a Native American hair stylist, resist the scalping jokes. Apparently that's still a touchy subject. The more you know....

Why do I have to put up with foreign music in taxis?

You don't. I set those road lizards straight as soon as I sit down. I recognize it is your cab and your business, but I'm leasing this bitch for the next twelve blocks. If you have the balls to charge me fourteen bucks per mile, then we ain't listening to Mohammad's greatest hits along the way.

Oh, and while we are on the subject, Mr. Middle-Eastern Cabbie, I appreciate the effort at cultural understanding, but forty-seven pine-scented car trees does not a bath make.

Are hookers really prevalent in Europe?

Seriously? They are everywhere. If that's your thing, have fun. If not, just make sure you don't get roped into some seedy after-hours place where the first drink is free and then next costs you a kidney. Luckily, the ladies are, at their core, business people. They know repeat customers are more valuable than one-time Johns, and the college-aged voyeurs aren't worth the pole-dance-inspired calluses.

Case in point: once, while sitting at an outside café in Germany, this old broad approached me and began rattling on in that Klingon-like excuse for a language. After a moment, a look of understanding washed over her face and she said, "Americano?"

I nodded and she repeated enthusiastically, "Yes, yes, Americano."

JACKSON HOLIDAY

"Do you speak English?" I asked.

She took her turn to nod and then asked, with full arm motion mind you, if I wanted to "Fuckie-fuckie."

She was eighty-seven years old for Chrissakes. Plus, her prices were really out of line. Damn exchange rates.

I'm not very worldly. How can I travel without embarrassing myself?

Americans are supposed to be loud, obnoxious, stupid and fat. That's our culture, and if other people can't embrace and respect that, well, then they are just being hypocritical.

I'm always making fun of other people, but I'm no genius either. Seriously, I just had to look up the word "genius" 'cause I always spell it "genious."

And my stupidity knows no geographical boundaries. For example, I had no idea where Geneva was before I went there. I mean I'd heard of the Geneva Convention and all, but I kinda thought it was a huge party room in Italy named after the salami. Man, I'm dumb. I can't believe I get published. I must be the only living illiterate author.

Don't sweat it, brother. Go forth, drink and frolic.

Are you a Republican or a Democrat?

Sorry, but I have a brain. No single political party or religion has enough on the ball for me to sign up for the free t-shirt. I like the middle ground and the opportunity it affords me to weigh things as they come, free of allegiances.

BAD ADVICE

In my experience, when you get more than five people involved in something, you'll have a hard time agreeing on a lunch location. Groups are bad. Causes are worse.

What's the most disturbing thing you've seen in your travels?

You'd think it would be raw sewage in the streets of India, the fly-filled faces of starving children in Africa or even the emotionally scarring donkey show in Thailand. But Sally Struthers and an eclectic porn collection slowly transformed those horrors into white noise. For me, the grossest grossness came on a city bus in Singapore.

As I sat idly listening to my iPod, this ancient sandal-clad savage bypassed an uncharacteristically empty vehicle and sat directly across from me. We acknowledged each other's presence with a nod, and then the maniac proceeded to remove his footwear and trim his wolverine-like talons. I sat there aghast, thinking this image could not get any worse. Then, as if fate had heard my unspoken declaration, a nail shot from the creature's foot and caught me an inch below the eye.

Being slightly (okay, *completely*) germ-phobic, I dashed from the bus, bolted to a drugstore and spent the evening bathing in peroxide. Great job, clipper head. Thanks to you and my psychological make-up I'm sporting a red, itchy torso, and a hooker-blonde hairdo. Work tomorrow will be fun for sure.

JACKSON HOLIDAY

Should I get a Eurorail pass?

Trains are cheap and plentiful, but they aren't exactly consistent country to country. For example, Spanish trains suck the sweat off a dead gorilla's balls. The French, on the other hand, may have faggotty food prepared by a kaleidoscope of cowards, but they make a helluva locomotive.

If you have the means and you're not just bouncing city to city, fly. If you're broke, local or just killing time before college, at least be smart about your seat selection. Play your cards right and you may find yourself cuddled up to a transient, hostel-bound hottie.

Does cool translate across cultures?

In Vienna I saw a group of teenage girls proudly sporting Burger King crowns as if they were some Fifth Avenue fashion. The guys they were snogging strutted about in Converse, tight purple jeans and cut-off sweatshirts that seemed to have come right off the rack of some *Flash Dance* reunion party.

Cool is a myth. It always has been. Be yourself with attitude and people will deal. If not, screw 'em. Chances are they are just doofuses in disguise.

How do foreign military leaders get their ranks?

Well, that's random. You are aware that there is an invention called Google and I'm not it, right?

Look, I'm in no mood to craft a dissertation on the matter, but since you asked, the simple answer is that they usually secure the titles

BAD ADVICE

through a combination of brute force and bullshit.

Take Colonel Gaddafi, for example. In the real world, Gaddafi is to Colonel what Captain is to Crunch. Bassackward and nonsensical. Don't fret, though. The guy could have selected any title he wanted and he went with middle management. Why not opt for Corporal Klinger? At least then we could make the crazy connection.

Why do foreigners paint ceilings?

In olden times, before the evolution of actual medicine, a bunch of hookers, potion-concocting holy men and chiropractors got together to dream up a dastardly bit of dickery that would increase business for the lot of them. The result was ceiling art. The naked models made people horny, the related sinning made them guilty, and all the contorted coupling left them with some wicked kinks.

- **A Related Note:** The scary part is that before long this reasoning will wind up on Wikipedia and thus, in some eighth grader's essay.

I don't get Europe. How can people live so close and disagree so strongly?

I take it you were an only child.

Look, disagreements, be they between siblings or countries, often stem from a simple difference of perspective. For example, it can be said that the Germans will look at a situation and note that it is serious, but not hopeless. The Austrians, on the other hand, are apt to view the same circumstances and conclude that it is indeed hopeless, but not serious. That slight difference in outlook can change everything around it. The world is a complicated place, but I assure you, if it wasn't, it would suck boring's balls.

- **A Not Entirely Related Note:** If you want to leave the planet, but don't have a spaceship, go to Japan. Just be sure to bring a fist-full of yen and a sense of humor. The only familiar things are the power outlets.

What are your thoughts on green energy?

Let's break this one down into bite-size chunks of stupid, shall we?

- **Wind:** You'd likely gain more power by collecting the flatulence from a single Chicago Bears fan than all the windmills in northern California. These dust-collecting eyesores become less efficient with each revolution. Why not hook the power grid up to my grandmother's peddle loom? No. Wait. This idea works...for the power needs of a small Amish community.
- **Solar:** Unless you are planning to harness the sun's power directly a la *Superman IV*, you are basically wasting your time. Solar panels are cumbersome and expensive and are as attractive as a 300-pound ballerina in a size three tutu. And, as the great Lex Luthor came to realize, nothing solar powered works at night, dickwad.
- **Clean Coal:** Slightly more attractive than date rape, this euphemistic oxymoron is proof that advertising works and people are sheep. What, are you planning to give each hunk a bubble bath before blasting its burnt carcinogenic waste into the

BAD ADVICE

atmosphere? Install the scrubbers if it makes you feel better, but it's hard to put a positive spin on black lung and Chinese slave labor.

Is global warming real?

The hippies call it "climate change" now. Global warming was big deal a while back, until we had a few *freeze your balls off* winters. Now anytime there's a weather change more dramatic than a late-night burrito fart, the crazies claim we're headed for Armageddon. In fairness, I'm sure we're fucked, but take heart, my socially conscious Care Bear. I'm sure we'll kill ourselves off via some embarrassing mishap long before the environment thing becomes an issue. I'm thinking the global equivalent of sticking one's pecker in the electric socket.

But seriously ...

There are two primary tasks associated with travel, especially business travel: trying to fall asleep and trying to stay awake. I've never been good at either, but the hassle is worth it. It's a big, beautiful world, and it would be a shame to live a lifetime in a single location. So get out there and look around. The view is nothing compared to the company you'll encounter.

Still, sometimes I think the best part of travel is the journey home, knowing that despite all you've learned, the most important lesson is realizing how much you miss those you've left behind. Maybe that's why people seem so goofy at airports. It's an honest, if not fleeting, feeling. A hug that ends too quickly, lost in the wake of excitement that becomes our normalcy.

JACKSON HOLIDAY

Spiritual Well-Being
*****

"Assuming that there is a heaven, who would ever want to go there? Ya know? I mean think about it; it's cool, you're sitting there up on this cloud. It's nice. It's quiet. There's no teachers, there's no parents ... but guess what ... there's nothing to do! It's fucking boring!"
– Christian Slater as Mark Hunter in *Pump Up the Volume*

*****

The trouble with me, I suppose, is that I was true Gen-X latchkey kid. By the time my parents got around to discussing religion I had already seen *Star Wars.* If taken at face value — outside social pressure and cultural norms — Yoda is a hell of a lot more believable than Jesus.

Let's review. On one hand you have a passive yet powerful Force that connects all things and provides an opportunity for continued existence and personal development. On the other you have a virgin-born, robe-wearing, sandal-sporting hippie who lacked the people skills to avoid getting nailed to a block of wood.

Star Wars alleged that if you worked hard and made moral choices you could become a righteous Jedi Knight, have plenty of like-minded friends, save hot chicks in woe, and go on some kick-ass adventures. Catholicism noted that if you prayed constantly, resisted the temptation to jerk off, and confess your sins to a collar-clad creepster in a box, you might not burn for all eternity.

In truth, they had me at light saber. I've diligently reevaluated my selection each year over the past few decades, but oddly enough, telekinesis still seems more believable than building the universe in six days. I'm no Monsignor, but I'm sure construction permits are hard to come by in any dimension.

I thought it best you know my frame of reference before I commence with the advice-giving.

How often should I pray?

Lighten up on the monologues, would ya? Prayer is like spamming God. Ladies, I'm sure he would get around to solving world hunger, but you are cluttering his inbox with messages about that extra five pounds and why Jimmy doesn't like you. Hint: I'm sure it has something to do with a lack of blowjobs.

Guys, you are no better. God isn't a bookie. We haven't talked in a while, but I'm sure he doesn't give two shits about the over-under on the Steelers game.

Do you think there is a devil?

Yes. We play racquetball on Thursdays. His existence doesn't disturb me as much as his backhand and the fact that he sports a soul patch. That level of irony kinda makes the whole religion thing feel like a sham.

JACKSON HOLIDAY

If reincarnation exists, wouldn't people who were unhappy with their current circumstances just off themselves and start over?

I'd imagine that the soothing philosophy of reincarnation and the harsh reality of suicide are two very different things.

You could argue, of course, that both are like recycling newspaper — a little pulp-producing give-and-take from the forest of existence. Still, my guess is that there's a dark side to that production process. Let's say you wimp out and do the deed with a fistful of sleeping pills. That's painless. But you're forgetting the fine print. Most people aren't bothered by the actual death. What really gives people pause is the sobering thought that, once complete, they may not remember yesterday's headlines.

My family is convinced I'm going to hell because I got divorced. How can I help them see it's not the end of the world?

The only difference between heaven and hell is the population and your point of view. My guess is that, regardless of who is right, you'll end up where you most want to be. So enjoy the ride and the destination, whatever it turns out to be.

Why do they make you swear on a Bible in court? What happened to separation of church and state?

Let me get this straight. You are looking for common sense from the government and religious institutions? Yeah, good luck with that. Still, some progress has been made recently. For example, North Carolina will now let you swear on any religious text you want when testifying in open court.

Bravo. Good show. Jews, Muslims, Taoists, etc. can now all commit perjury via their most sacred writings. Of course the atheists will complain — you know, the sarcastically inclined fellows who tout that God is likely an imaginary friend for grownups — something akin to Santa in summer clothes. These folks are still faced with a dim, though thankfully broader, selection of literary adventures from which to choose. Perhaps they could be allowed to swear upon a compilation of Darwin's greatest hits or a good Richard Bach novel. Now that would be nifty.

Hello? Hell? Yes, a reservation for two... No. No. Something by the kitchen would be fine.

What should I give up for lent?

I'm not exactly Father Guido Sarduci, but my question is, why are you only giving up one thing? What are you, a wimp?

Let me introduce you to a little concept called Super Lent. Last year some friends and I were discussing this topic over drinks. Well, as beer turned to shots and twos turned to tens, we started piling on the list of vices and daring each other to commit to forty days of straight living. This soon turned into a high-stakes wager, winner take all.

The challenge? Here is a run-down of items on the table. 1. Fast food, 2. Red meat, 3. Alcohol, 4. Soda, 5. Coffee and tea, 6. Sex with AND without a partner, 7. Dating, 8. Porn, 9. Complaining, 10. Non-work-related web crawling, 11. Cursing, and 12. TV. (We went with twelve things to appease our one Jewish friend. Freakin' Hebrews.

The deal was whoever lasted the longest won the pot and (via a little negotiation with Jesus), forgiveness for two years' worth of hardcore sinning. Of course, since I'm not a religious guy, this endeavor can only be described as the most cataclysmically stupid thing I've ever done.

- **A Related Note:** Screw that Atkins bastard, body by Super Lent is the way to go. Two weeks in and I lost some serious poundage.
- **Another Related Note:** Okay, after like an hour of Super Lent, you realize it's hard to give up things like red wine and jerking off. So for each transgression you have to do fifty pushups. According to a recent amendment, this keeps you in the pool and further aligns you to the path of hotness. The hope being, of course, that at some point you can actually have sex with another person.

I feel like life is moving too fast. How can I slow down?

Time doesn't pass you by. You experience every second. Want it to slow down? Go to the dentist, stand in a bank line, or visit your mother-in-law.

Do humans and modern primates share a common evolutionary ancestor?

Yes, I believe it is called Alabama.

Alabama people, please don't write me with snarky retorts. I could have said Kentucky, Georgia or a host of square states. Lighten up.

BAD ADVICE

- **A Related Note:** I wasn't sure what they officially called people from Alabama – Alabamions, Alabamanites. Not a clue. And so in the spirit of the techo generation I posed the question to Google. The search results yielded a few redneck references, some black jokes and a reference to Paul Simon's "You Can Call Me Al". This, my friends, is why I rarely research anything.

Is one religion better than others?

I find that people know amazingly little about their own religion, never mind enough to make that assumption. Besides, organized religion is to God what tax law is to poetry.

What's a praise team?

Is someone trying to bang the hot, fundamentalist intern? Look, let me save you some heartache. If a bright, blonde, perky twenty-something mentions a mission trip, she's probably not referring to a beer run. Praise teams are like cheerleaders for Jesus. Think band camp without all the relative coolness. (And no, there's no game of hide-the-flute in Bible study.) These chicks are harder to seduce than a militant, butch lesbian at a Harley convention. And trust me, you don't want to succeed with either party.

How do you read a hymnal?

Well, let me ask you this, Sparky. Can you read? Be honest.

Okay, phonic-boy, I'll take you at your word. So here's the deal. A hymnal is like the sound track for the Bible.

JACKSON HOLIDAY

It's pretty easy to follow. Even your allegedly literate ass can pull it off. Most of the songs are the same. You know, "Praise God in the highest, holy, holy, holy Lord..." that sort of thing. If you get confused, just throw in a couple of hallelujahs, something about a sheep, and an amen. You should be okay.

- **A Related Note:** This works even better in black Baptist churches, especially down south. If you ever flub a line, just go apeshit and start rejoicing. People go nuts for a good spiritual awakening and if you done-did see the light, all is usually forgiven.
- **Another Note:** I'm not sure where they are getting these musical holy men, but church singing sucks more than a three a.m. karaoke session in Chinatown. If you ever need to increase your confidence for an *American Idol* audition, head down to your local synagogue. If you can't out-sing some ancient Hebrews, you're just wasting three days on line and no one really wants to be in a blooper video.

Why are religious people so serious?

I think it is the hell thing. They just need to close their eyes and think of Christmas. Everyone loves Christmas, even the Chinese. After all, they get big business from the Jews and the culinarily challenged.

You see, the truth is that Jesus is Santa for adults. Prayers are Christmas letters. Coal is hell and presents heaven. Give the messiah a sandwich, a suit and a sense of humor and religion would be tolerable.

BAD ADVICE

Is Scientology real? I've read some literature recently and it seems compelling.

First off, how's your Amway business going?

Listen, tard monkey, scientology is a bullshit thing. How do I know? A science *fiction* writer created it. Seriously, this guy's resume includes such titles as *Battlefield Earth*, *An Alien Affair*, and *Black Genesis*, which I haven't read, but just seems racist.

I'll admit that part of my distaste stems from pure, unadulterated jealousy. First off, he was one prolific fucker. The crazy bastard could pump out a pulp fiction book in the time it takes me to jot a questionably witty line on a greeting card. Second, the guy had balls. I can't imagine mustering the gumption to invent a religion and elect myself savior or at least el presidente. Hats off to you, Hubby.

"Wait a minute. Is that you, God? What? Zen-snark-o-tology is the one true path to enlightenment? But I thought that whole Jesus thing and the guy with the Ark.... Bullshit? Really? You don't say? And I need to spread the word? Okay, I'll get cracking. Of course, I'll need a little start-up capital. Not for me, no...for the church.

Sure, sure you help those who help themselves, but I'm sorta helping you on this one. Plus, you know, I have that pesky corporate gig.

Oh, great idea. We co-write a third book...maybe do some speaking engagements. Of course, you'll get top billing. No need to diva it up already. Jesus...oh sorry.

Look, hey, gotta run. I'm sort of in the middle of a paragraph here. Conference call next week? Maybe do some brainstorming...sketch out an outline? Great. How do I... Right, right. You'll call me. Fantastic.

See there, sheep kabob. The truth you were seeking will be out in paperback in a few months. Since I'm sure you will be a loyal serf, I mean disciple, I'll give you a little preview of the major plot points. First, if you wish to reach the final level (kind of like Bruce Leroy did in *The Last Dragon*) don't do anything douchey like buy complex Starbucks products or bootleg copies of this book. Second, try not to jack monkey up your chosen profession. If you suck at what you do, quit and try something else. The Great and Powerful Frank (that's "Lord" to you) hates incompetence. Finally, go out and get yourself laid. Membership has its privileges, after all.

Now that *has* to be better than subjecting yourself to a hippie-induced psychological audit in the hopes that some timeless, transcendental, intergalactic spirit will date rape you into a higher thetan level. Or, you know, something along those lines.

- **A Related Note:** Just for the record, a pamphlet some hippie handed you at a tent revival meeting doesn't count as *literature*. Steinbeck is literature. Tolstoy is literature. Heck, the local phone book has a more legitimate claim to the descriptor than the random ramblings of some ascot-sporting mental case.

How much should I give to my televangelist?

Um ... I'm going to go with nothing. Not a freakin' cent.

Why? Well, first off the pastor, preacher, hallelujah-shouting personable prick in question is actually on television. This means he already has more money, power and influence than some bathrobe-clad trailer dweller like you will ever muster. If anything, he should be sending you some monetary-enforced soul saving.

If you're actually concerned about the welfare of others, go direct. Head to the local homeless shelter and cough up a donation, or better yet, lend a hand. This way you can be sure your money and time arrive at the intended destination. They say God works in mysterious ways, but the only thing confusing about a suit-sporting preacher is how he can afford to drape himself in Armani. I haven't been to church in a while, but I don't remember Father Carmine wearing a Rolex.

Do you believe in the power of prayer?

Is that at all like the Power of the Home Depot? Or perhaps the power of the Dark Side of the Force? Either way, I think it would be more powerful if it had the bass timbre of James Earl Jones.

Why do I have to say "God bless you" when someone sneezes?

It's called conditioning. You know, like that guy with the bell and the salivating dogs. Western society picked up the custom a while back and soon the nicety turned into a habit. These days it's such a part of the expected social norm that even hardcore atheists find themselves absentmindedly issuing the sentiment.

The good news is that it's fixable. I've trained myself to shout "Go blow yourself!" any time someone sneezes in my general direction. The action helps on two fronts. First, it rids me of the implied social contract and ultimately futile religious action. And second, it stifles the sick to silence, thus sparing me from germs during the dastardly cold and flu season. Actually, now that I think of it, people rarely sneeze around me anymore. Way to go, Pavlov.

Do religious people ever swear?

Of course, but it depends on the setting. Bend a Catholic schoolgirl over a desk during detention and you'll hear some pretty creative cursing. Spill red wine on a white carpet in your Jewish friend's house and his grandmother will likely blurt out a barrage of profanity so perverse that your average teamster would blush and bolt for a more pious location. I'm not sure if Muslims blaspheme, since you never really know what the hell they're talking about, but you have to assume the occasional bomber belts a "fuck me" or an "oh shit" moments before the jerry-rigged jihad-maker does its business.

On a typical day I think the Mormons and those crazy-ass born-again bastards keep it clean. Though one holy-roller friend of mine admitted that her family uses a series of replacement words like "flarg" for the F-bomb when they need to make a point or have hot monkey sex. They even go so far as to work out the conjugation: flarg, flarged, flarging, and flargulous, which I don't fully understand.

In the end I don't think it matters much. As an ... ahem ... writer, I like to pride myself on having a relatively decent vocabulary. That said, sometimes cock-knocker is exactly the right word ... yes, questionable hyphen and all.

But seriously...

I don't go in for all this religious nonsense. I understand people believing in God, but religion, in my opinion, is a social evil. Sure, you can toss a few bucks in the basket and envision your donation reaching some black-and-white Victorian-style orphanage circa 1842, where, through your kindness, Sunday gruel now has a meat-like substance and a side of greens. But you're just kidding yourself.

Religious institutions provide charitable services like other nonprofits. The catch is the secular ones do so without a boatload of destructive dogma that in essence challenges nonbelievers to a schoolyard smack-down.

Drink the Kool-Aid if it makes you happy. Just know that organizations by design come complete with agendas, politics and administrative dickery. Hell a round of golf has all that, or so I'm told.

If I had to pick a spiritual guide, well, I'd like to meet a teenage Yoda. I bet he'd be reckless, a dreamer, a playful un-master. The force would be with him, and so would I. May it be with you as well, for there is no greater good than simply wishing another well.

JACKSON HOLIDAY

Family Matters
*****

"Happiness is having a large, loving, caring, close-knit family in another city." — George Burns

*****

In the spirit of full disclosure, I think it important to note that you are about to take family advice from a single, socially awkward, middle-aged man-boy who once gave his fourteen-year-old niece a straight-edge razor and a six-pack of duct tape for her birthday. In my defense, I was coming directly from the airport and those were the least offensive items I had in my trunk.

I get the concept of family. Apparently it's a group of allegedly blood-related people whom you can't sell on the black market and whom you must loan money to, pretend to listen to, and occasionally have dinner with. In return for the loans and listening, they also agree not to sell you into slavery while you sleep and will likely not kick you to the curb on the off chance that you get hit by a shit wagon and can no longer pen snarky literature. As far as the reality of family, I'm not as sure. Thus, my views may be slightly askew. Take heart and grab a helmet.

BAD ADVICE

The wife and I are thinking of having kids. We're both thirty, but busy with work. Is this the right time?

I'm completely lost when it comes to the wee ones, my friend. In my opinion, kids should be crafted in test tubes on some remote island research laboratory. I haven't studied the pregnancy process up close, but as I understand it, the only results are hemorrhoids, mood swings and "baby weight" fatness that never fully goes away. Plus, you end up with a kid, and that's no picnic — or so I'm told.

Since you've already ignored my counsel on marriage and taken the plunge, I can only assume you'll dick-monkey this wisdom as well. And so, breed if you must, but my advice is to put it off as long as possible. People say there is never a right time to have a kid. But there is, assuming you're a guy. That age is sixty-four.

If you're like me, God will punish you with hot, bisexual triplets. Best you die long before they date, which these days seems to start at age twelve. Plus, you get out of paying for college, which is nice.

Why are kids so friggin' fat?

I blame the school system. 'Cause, you know, why not?

You see, I have road rage. There, I said it. Step one is in the books. Actually, as someone who once had more points on his license than he had on the SAT, I feel I've made some significant personal progress. Still, something happened yesterday as I made my daily 6:30 a.m. drive from gym to job that nearly caused a relapse into reckless road-warrior mode. I got stuck behind a friggin' school bus.

Surely not the end of the world, you say, but wait, did I mention that it stopped every ten feet to let on what could best be described as a grungy band of Oompa Loompas?

Look, I'm not completely out of the loop. I've cast a pod, twitted a tweet, and even battled a twelve-year-old Chinese kid for global supremacy at 3 a.m., courtesy of X-Box live. Still, there are some old school pastimes that need to be, well, passed on. Look, I'm just spit-ballin' here, but since the president is throwing the cash around, how about we fund a little more gym time or some non-virtual team sports. In the meantime, let's space out those bus stops so kids can slim down and I can stay out of prison.

I know I should go to my kid's game, but my job is a killer. How can I make him understand?

Most people say their work is never done. Try as they might, there is always something on the desk. Funny that our play is not subject to the same thoughtful commitment. Our games have halves, whistles and umpires. Time is watched carefully and rarely extended. Fun has no extra innings and somehow the fat lady always sings. Perhaps she could lend her voice to the work world for a while.

Of course, till the singing starts you could always opt to focus on the important things. Jobs and bosses come and go, but family, whether we like it or not, tends to stick around. So do yourself a favor: make the game and forgo the therapy bills. Shrinks are some pricey bastards and, as far as I know, there's still no 529 savings plan for future psychiatric care.

Do you ever get over losing a family member?

A few years ago, my grass guy quit ... or was deported. I never got the actual story. Anyway, I attempted, foolishly, to complete the job on my own. Of course, since I have no skills, I struggled to start the mower and ultimately resorted to what I imagined was a normal troubleshooting procedure — cursing, screaming and hitting it repeatedly with a hammer.

Secure in my uselessness, I thought better of employing a blowtorch and instead walked to the kitchen to call my grandfather. He had a habit of tinkering with things and would undoubtedly be able to talk me through the issue in a minute or two. Anyway, as I stood with a ringing phone in my hand, I suddenly realized that he had died nearly a decade before.

I hung up quickly and smiled at my stupidity. Then I felt sad and guilty about not having shown as much interest as I should have when he was around. He was a great man who longed to teach me the little things every guy should know and that now, sadly, I do not.

I miss him, of course. And perhaps that's the bad news. You never quite shake losing someone you love. But in a way that's also the good news. They never fully leave.

I still had to hire a new grass guy and, at forty bucks a pop, that kinda sucks. Still, it's balls hot outside and I'm sitting on my ass drinking a beer. Ah, the circle of life.

JACKSON HOLIDAY

My son is growing up too fast. I want him to study and get into a good school, but I also want him to have fun. Any way to help him see the balance?

This is a tough one. The transition from kid to adult doesn't happen slowly. It's a sudden thing, with clear end points. We wake up one day and childhood is over. It's the moment that we stop jumping in puddles. You never know when it occurs, but it does and it's brutal. If it were up to me I'd save the soul and soil the pants.

Perhaps a way to make your case is to hop in the car one late afternoon and head to the local ball field. Kids will be playing for sure and the fun will be no surprise. But for one of them, that will be his last game. The last time he thinks that spending a day in play is time well spent. If your son hasn't reached that point, it's a reminder to savor the moments. If he has, get your ass out of the car and toss the baseball about. Nothing slows time like conversation and a game of catch.

My sister is having a baby, her first. I want to be there, but I'm out of the country. What should I do?

Write a "Welcome to Earth" letter. I did the same a while back and it's become a keepsake. Here's a sample.

Dear Monkey Boy,

Welcome to Earth. Douglas Adams described it as "mostly harmless," but we'll get to your required reading list later.

Right about now, you're probably being bombarded with a series of oohs and ahs as excited family members nervously pass you

BAD ADVICE

about. Grown-ups really dig that whole baby-talk thing. If they're still doing it when you're eight, up their meds.

Anyway, I'm your Uncle Jackson, a wholly remarkable guy who you will no doubt come to love and admire ... but all in due time. For now, think of me as the planet's maître d'. I have no official power, but can swing the proverbial floor seats while steering you clear of such horrors as strained Brussels sprouts, disco and waitresses named Cookie (again, all in due time). Anyway, since I can't goo and gaa with the rest of the gang, let me at least give you the low-down on your situation. Simply put, you lucked out, kiddo.

First off, you landed in America. Trust me on this one, as I've danced across most of the planet. This is the place to be. There is no challenge ahead that can't be bested with a little ingenuity and a lot of hard work. Yes, here you can do whatever you dream. So dream big.

Next, you have an awesome family. They're funny, warm and a little crazy, but, despite their quirks (and oh my, do we have some quirks!) you'll always have a corner full of supporters when you climb into the ring.

As for parents, well, your dad is hysterical — some of the best dry wit I've ever heard. Soak that up if you can. I don't know him as well as others, to be sure, but one thing I really dig about the guy is that he always does what he says he'll do. Even-tempered, wicked smart ... he's someone you can always count on, and that's not as common as one might think.

Your mom? ... well, I know you haven't had an opportunity to acquaint yourself with a Swiffer yet, but just don't fall for the old, "no, really son,

JACKSON HOLIDAY

a four-wheel, off-road, nuclear-powered vacuum-cleaner is just like a bicycle." When you get to be about six I'll start the "act real stupid so you don't get chores" lessons. It worked for me. Seriously, you hit the jackpot in the mom department. And I'm not just saying that 'cause she scares me. She is hysterical, brilliant and can bake a cookie like nobody's business. Plus, she knows how to listen — really listen — and has a great way of putting things in perspective so you can make the most of your choices.

Now, you'll get a lot of advice throughout life, mostly 'cause it's free. So I'll bite my tongue for now other than to say, enjoy the ride.

Anyway, I'm sorry I couldn't be there for your big day, but I'll see you soon enough. In the meantime, take it easy on the folks for a while — they'll be a wreck. And try not to barf on anyone, unless of course it's Uncle Jay. He owes me money.

I can't seem to connect with kids. What am I doing wrong?

My guess, you're trying too hard.

You can cracks jokes, ease up on the "good advice" (*It's like ray-e-ain on your wedding day*) or strive to be the cool older guy that really "gets" these kids today. The trouble is, you're not cool and you don't get them. Seriously, you're not. You don't. And that's okay.

Kids understand beatings, hugs and honest efforts. Choose the right mix and you'll earn more than a simple connection.

BAD ADVICE

Should we adopt a cat?

We've been through this. Cats are evil, sneaky little fur fuckers. And the ones at the shelter are pure, unfiltered propaganda machines. Seriously, when the hell did these animals achieve literacy? I mean, there's no way the employees are scripting the felines' *Lifetime*-like tale of woe. Half of them are homeless, on parole, and/or rocking a fifth-grade reading level. It's got to be the cats. You've seen the commercials. They use the first person, for Christ's sake.

"Hi. My name is Fluffy and I'm a cute, cuddly kitten who just needs the love of a good home."

Bullshit. I can read between the lines, fur ball. What you really need is a leather couch to scratch, a carpet to piss on and a sucker who will ultimately adopt fourteen of your brothers and sisters. Seriously, you breed faster than an Irish Mormon at Woodstock.

Beware of advertising, folks. No good can come from it.

My wife and I are over, really over. Should we stay together for the kids?

No. First off, they probably never liked you. Second, it's just stupid. Kids have a sixth sense when it comes to dysfunction. You're not going to put anything over on them, so forget the charade. Best you split and negotiate a reasonable custody arrangement before things get ugly.

No one likes divorce, but kids will respect the honesty ... when they're older, of course. In the meantime, it will be tough, but at least with free nights you have a shot at getting laid. And sex just keeps everyone in a better state of mind.

JACKSON HOLIDAY

How can I tell my parents I'm gay?
Start rollerblading. They'll get the message.

I'm really disappointed in my parents. It's not like they're losers. They're just so normal. Should I say anything?
It's a funny time in your life when you realize that parents are people; people no better or worse than any other. When the pendulum of admiration and resentment swings to the center, you have friendship. Go with that, and build from there.

Who knows? They might surprise you. From the letters I've received, chances are they're into swinging, S&M and recreational weed.

What is the most effective way to discipline a child?
These days, parents are big fans of the "time out." We had those when I was a kid; they just called them "beatings."

Now let me clarify before I get sued ... again. I'm not saying you should crack the little bastard across the face with a monkey wrench if he refuses to eat his strained peas, but a little fear of God, Yoda or the great and powerful Frank is a good tool to have in your arsenal.

Negotiating with a two-year-old is about as productive as using win-win discourse to navigate the Middle-East peace process. Neither party really understands the other. And, if asked in an honest moment, both would probably prefer a nice juice box to the item they've been arguing over.

In the end you're the boss. Act like it, Susan.

BAD ADVICE

Do bumper stickers reduce a car's value? I ask because my son earned a new "my kid's a scholar" sticker and I need to decide which vehicle to put it on.

It's times like this when I wish this was a pop-up book. The only challenge would be whether the page would shoot you the bird or punch you in the dick.

Are you mentally ill? I'm not sure whether to comment on the car-related incompetence or the idle douchebaggary associated with your offspring management. No matter, assuming he wasn't adopted or the wife wasn't banging the mailman, it's safe to say that junior will end up working at the car wash. So go ahead, bumper-stick away. Congratulations, you're a job creator.

I hate my in-laws. They are old, crotchety and annoying. Any advice on dealing with them?

Depends on how much you are looking to spend and whether it needs appear like an accident. Couples are tricky, of course, 'cause you eliminate the main suspect. My advice is to simply off one and frame the other. Problem solved, and you save money. Sound thinking during a recession, if you ask me.

I think my daughter might be having sex. She's fourteen. What do I do?

First, punch yourself in the face. You suck as a parent. Second, buy a chainsaw and find out where those horny little fuckers live. You've got some killing to do.

*****

JACKSON HOLIDAY

Okay, wait, I've calmed down a bit. You're still a shitty parent, but I'm no longer having a cardiac arrest.

Look, the topic is difficult because people by nature are insecure. No, scratch that. Nature has nothing to do with it. Babies are pretty freaking secure. So are toddlers and the majority of four-year-olds I've come in contact with. People don't start developing body issues and making poor choices until they start comparing themselves to swimsuit models and being teased by bitchy cool kids in grammar school.

This is why I recommend that children learn to fight. Other kids might be smarter, better looking or more talented, but nothing settles an argument faster than a punch in the throat. Plus, everyone understands violence. I'm not concerned with ensuring my daughter wins homecoming queen, but popular kids seem to still call the shots. If the path to coolness is a toll road, I'd rather her pay in skulls cracked over dicks sucked any day. But then again, I'm old fashioned.

My twenty-nine-year-old brother still lives in my basement. How long do I have to support him?

Says in your letter that Johny Rotten is waiting the occasional table while he pursues his dream of reviving America's passion for polka. Look, I hate to be the one to crush a dream, but it's time to get all Simon Cowell on his buttocks.

You seem like a sucker (by the way, thanks for the check), so it's doubtful you'll heed my initial advice and kick him to the curb. A softer sell is to set a deadline — perhaps his thirtieth birthday?

BAD ADVICE

If he hasn't made it by then, he needs to pay his own way. Not sure what kind of family guilt you have going, but you need to shake the daddy complex and make the little bird fly on his own.

You can do everything for a friend except make him do for himself. It's time for you both to man up and stand on your own. That said, my imaginary gopher needs an appendix transplant. Would you mind kicking in a grand or two for the procedure? Thanks, man. Oh, and I appreciate you letting your wife tutor me. The professor for my online female anatomy course says the oral final exam will be a tough job.

But seriously ...

Sometimes I feel we over-think things. There are so many psychologists, self-help books and TV gurus telling you want to think, feel and say. But I'm not sure we need all the chatter. People have been having families since Adam and Eve allegedly got it on toga-style in Great Garden Gone Wrong. And sure, there were a lot of kin-related missteps as we marched through time. But humans are still here and that says something. Mostly it proves that the majority of the population still can't properly unroll a condom. But that's another matter.

Family is a fairly simple affair. Keep your sons out of prison. Prevent your daughters from turning tricks for an eight ball of blow. And keep your in-laws safely secured in another state. Do that while managing to pay your bills and you have a head start on most of the planet's population.

There will be challenges along the way. From cyber bullies to cancer scares. But most times the good outweighs the bad. And in truth, even the hardest cynic will admit that it's nice to have some folks in your corner when the shit hits the fan.

BAD ADVICE

Sex: You Know, 'Cause It's Fun
*****
"Just look inside yourself and you'll see me waving up at you naked wearing only a cock ring."
— Christian Slater as Mark Hunter in *Pump Up the Volume*

*****

Like many American males, most of my early sexual experiences came via some unscented hand lotion and a Sears catalog. This might seem pathetic, but in fairness my formative years preceded the invention of the Internet. I'm certain that if access had been available I would have rubbed a few out to a midget lesbian snuff film, but alas I had to make do with the granny panty models in the underwear section. The thought that this is now a legitimate fetish with no fewer than twelve websites devoted to this old-school spank genre is quite disturbing.

I've learned a bit since the whack-off days. Not much, admittedly, but based on the questions I've received, enough to dazzle many of your wives and girlfriends ... and perhaps a few of your sheep.

Jackson, how do I find the clitoris?
What I do is take the Taconic Parkway south to Exit 347, hang a left and floor it.

Forget the clitoris, you putz. I'm pretty sure that's just something chicks made up so they could keep us on our toes. And even if it does exist, you shouldn't feel obligated to go on a recon mission just cause she can't get herself off. Just because there is a fundamental design flaw with the female anatomy doesn't mean you have to play an hour-long game of Marco Polo with your girlfriend's chooch. My advice, get a map or a hooker.

I just can't seem to get laid. What's wrong with me?

Nothing that a few thousand pushups and a lobotomy wouldn't fix, I bet.

Seriously, I know what it's like to go through a dry spell. There was a time back in college when if I hadn't had to pee, I swear my dick would have had cobwebs on it. I actually pitched an idea for a TV series called *Quest for Sex*, but alas it was before the reality-show boom. I missed my window in more ways than one, I guess.

But back to you. Stop worrying about women. It says here you are from Alabama. If things don't turn around, there's always livestock and family members. Chin up, bucko.

Guys always say they "need" to get laid, but are there any physical repercussions to not having sex?

I'm actually a bit stunned that this question would come from someone who can properly spell the word 'repercussions'. You must be religious.

While there are no physical issues, not getting laid for an extended period of time can wreck havoc with one's mental condition. Here are some subtle signs that your boyfriend may need some booty:*

BAD ADVICE

- He finds himself strangely turned on in the produce section of the supermarket. (Think melons.)
- He's actively following the acting careers of the performers in the Cinemax skin flicks.
- He gets a woody reading *Field and Stream*.
- He's seriously contemplating going to a sexaholics meeting to find out what they are doing right.
- He thinks his best shot of getting near vagina is to become a "born again" Christian.
- He watches *The Simpsons* and thinks, "Marge? Yeah, I'd do her."
- He gets hard when someone blows their nose.
- He's purchased 347 boxes of Girl Scout cookies in hopes that they will remember him in eight years.
- His right hand is freakishly toned and the rest of him is slowly morphing into a soft, jelly-like substance.
- He spends his spank-o-licious downtime writing obscure lists for an awesome sequel to *Who Shit in My Zen Garden?* (Oh wait, now that's embarrassing.)

*Based on many moons of introspection and a grant from the friendly people at *Sesame Street*.

I never thought I'd say this, but I'm thinking of cheating on my wife. I love her, but I'm just not attracted to her anymore. Should I get some on the side?

You are being a chicken shit in that you want to eat your cake and have it too. If you go through with the dastardly deed, at least be safe. Just

remember, you can wrap your pecker, but they don't make condoms for the conscience.
- **A Related Note:** Everyone gets that cake saying wrong and it really pisses me off. Anyone can have their cake and then eat it. That's called dessert, you dick monkey. Eating your cake but still having it around is a tougher bit of business, assuming you're not bulimic. Sorry, supermodels and jockeys.

I think my girlfriend was a slut before we met. Should it bother me this much?

We all have a history. I have so many skeletons in my closet I once had Indiana Jones pop over for a dig. Only you will know if her number is a deal breaker. Sometimes our heaviest baggage is the emotional Samsonite we lug around. If you love the girl, check it at the curb.

I'm always horny, I mean really horny. Is there something wrong with me?

Nothing that some porn and a silo of K-Y Jelly won't fix. But take heart, you're not the only one. I once got so distracted by a flirting (in my imagination) Harris Teeter cashier that I hit the "opt for Spanish" button on the checkout screen. I'm not sure, but I think I paid $78.45 for a dozen eggs.

I don't think my husband is attracted to me anymore. Is there something I can do stoke the fire?

As a woman, you know that sex is all about the emotional intimacy two people share. My

BAD ADVICE

guess is that you stopped doing the little things that bring him closer to you. Try these ten tips for wowing him back into ramming you senseless.

1. Surprise him. Put away your liberal sensibilities and equal rights mantra long enough to make him a sandwich. You know he's usually hungry when he gets home stumbling drunk from a night out with the guys.
2. Try to remember that Sunday is football day. Learn the names of the players on his favorite team and impress him with your knowledge of why the play-offs are more important than a trip to your mother's.
3. Understand that beer makes him fart and farting is just a natural part of who he is. Don't be grossed out by a good game of turtle (ask if you have to) and please sit next to him when he's watching Caddyshack for the ninety-seventh time and floating butt bombs that could knock a buzzard off a shit wagon.
4. A blow job is nice, but letting him bang your hot semi-lesbian friend while you videotape it so his friends can see and call him "the man" is really thoughtful. Keep that in mind. Going overboard is the key to healthy relationships.
5. Understand guys' night by really buddying up to his friends. Say things like, "Hey, why not use my dad's lake house to have your friend's bachelor party. You know he's only on the forth step with AA and just can't say no to cold beer and cheap hookers. It'll be fun. I trust you. Besides, you're a man. You got needs."

6. Road-head any time after six months of dating really shows you're not going to let the relationship get stale. Show you care ... grab the *other* stick shift and send him into overdrive.
7. Think outfits. We don't want you naked. We want you mostly naked. Keep a stock of classic male-fantasy outfits (cheerleader, nurse, Mother Teresa...oops, did I type that out loud?) and figure out a way to keep it thirty percent on while he rams you against the fridge.
8. Realize that guys look. It's genetic, and as natural as farting. Blame Jesus if you must. But understand that it's going to happen. So if you make him visit your family, don't be pissed if he looks at your sister's ass (unless she is twelve). You brought him there. It's your fault.
9. Mow the lawn. You can do it. It's as easy as walking around. Do it after you make us food, invite our friends over and leave us to watch the game and you get double points. Want a triple word score? Mow the lawn with a hot friend, in an OUTFIT and then come in and both screw him in front of the gang.
10. Be thankful. If he picks up the check (again), offer a voucher for a future sexual misstep. You know, when he says something like, "I have no idea how my dick got in her. I was just watching the lesbian donkey show and then *bang*...one in a million."

BAD ADVICE

I love sex with new women, but when does my number cross the line?

An ex-girlfriend once said, "If you've been with everyone then everyone's been with you. So where does that leave us?"

I hate to get all after-school-special on you, but that kind of puts things in perspective. We all have a history: college flings, meaningful relationships and a few random backseat romps sprinkled into our sexual transcript. Really, it's hard to say what the ideal number is. Chances are, if you're twenty-five and flipping the ass odometer into the triple digits, you're just a big whore. Of course, at this point it's too late, so give me a call.

Would you ever date a girl who didn't shave?

Sorry, I don't speak French. Seriously, I'm sure Sasquatch has a lovely personality, but I'm not taking her to the prom.

Any tips for scoring at a wedding?

Forget the bridesmaids. Too much competition, and with people getting hitched later in life half of them are usually married already. My advice is to go for the chick in white.

Once the cake is cut, the toasts are toast and the reception gets into full swing, the recently wed is often, surprisingly, left to her own devices. Think about it. The groom is usually hammered and trying to enjoy the last night with his buddies that he'll see for a while. Or, in the case of an Italian wedding, he'll be so preoccupied with counting the cash gifts that he'll forget the chick's name.

JACKSON HOLIDAY

And not to worry about the bridesmaids. The single ones will be busy trying to bang the wait staff while the rest are often so angry about having to sport those ass-enlarging dresses that they'd probably root for you just for the revenge factor. Everything is filmed at weddings.

Your best bet for a little bride action is to strike at the exact moment when she realizes that she can't dance in a wedding dress and needs to head to the bridal suite to change. Snag her by the coat-check and offer to escort her up stairs... after all, navigating a spiral staircase in heels and a gown is tough enough before thirteen shots.

You'll get an "aw shucks" look, for sure. Women love that chivalry shit. If she's a ho bag, you'll probably nail her chick-dance style. Worst case, she'll put in a good word for you with the flower catchers. Everyone loves a referral.

I think my girlfriend is a bit of a tart. Any warning signs?

Um, does she currently have a penis in her mouth that is not yours? No? Well, that's good news.

Look, everyone has a past. Maybe she was a slut monkey before meeting you. Maybe she still is. My advice is to talk things through to the level of your mutual comfort and then make some decisions. If there is something in her past you really can't live with, better you know early on. As for the future: get tested, set your go-forward ground rules and then have fun.

- **A Related Note:** Ladies, clean house before the next contestant comes over. Safe sex is always a good idea, but no one likes to use the last guy's condoms. First of all,

BAD ADVICE

the Magnum thing is a bit optimistic, and second, those glow-in-the-dark jimmies are just awkward. I have enough pressure knowing your last boyfriend was hung like a T.rex. I really don't need my penis feeling like an accountant at a rave.

I'm not well endowed ... at all. Do I need to disclose this?

I tell women that I'm hung like an animal. Later on, if they happen to realize that I was referring to a hamster — well, the joke is on them. It's not my fault if they skimped on the research.

Having a tiny penis is enough of a hardship. No need to advertise. Get what you can until rumors reach a critical mass, and then move or invest in hookers. In the end, you'll appreciate the variety and the cost savings.

How do I know if it's love or just sex?

I'm not following you. Oh wait, sorry, just realized that the letter was from Nickie and not Nicky. I didn't get much in the way of scenario build, so let me give you some general guidelines.

If you talk about the future, go on actual dates and kiss extensively before and after the deed, chances are you're at least in the "like" stage. If, however, your couplings are in response to a series of two a.m. booty calls, you've yet to be seen in public together and at the end of the evening he reluctantly provides cab fare...well, in his mind, you are probably little more than a stigma-free prostitute.

JACKSON HOLIDAY

My girlfriend gave me a hickey, which, given our ages, seems sort of childish. How can I get her to chill out?

I feel for you, brother. Nothing says bush league (in a bad way) like walking into a conference room sporting a prepubescent love bite. Basically, you're screwed. Home remedies rarely work, turtlenecks don't fly in southern summers and everyone over the age of twelve knows the common excuses.

It happened to me once, and I offered my coworker some line of shit about a Krav Maga classes and a choke technique taken too far. Even with my martial arts background and a host of some pretty specific details, he still put his money on me banging an intern. He was spot-on, of course, but fuck me if that wasn't a creative cover.

My advice is to work from home on day one and then get the teenybopper to hook you up with some cover-up. If she's jumping your old bones, she's probably a pro.

- **A Related Note:** I once got a dick hickey. I didn't notice it at the time...mostly because I was being blown by a scantily clad grad-school hottie with Hoover-like suction and some serious staying power. Unfortunately, when I whipped out the wonder wand the next morning I took one look at my purple tool and nearly passed out in the urinal. Just another reason one should pay attention to the details.
- **Another Related Note:** While I agree with you on this one, in general you should just go with the flow. Love is a full-contact

sport. Stop bitching and buy a helmet. Trust me, the sex will be better.

How do I find the perfect mate?

What is this, *Wild Kingdom*? Unless you are a freakin' wildebeest cool it on the *mate* talk. First, it implies commitment. And second, well...it just freaks people out. Search for a girl with whom you can have a cup of coffee without wanting to strangle her. If that goes well, ask for a second date. If you play your cards right, you'll be on to the mating business in no time.

But seriously ...

Sex is weird, I suspect, because you have to... or at least in more traditional instances...get naked. The trouble with this is that most people are disgusting, and that puts a damper on the event.

When you are young, the people you fantasize about sleeping with are usually pretty hot. Either they are also young, which makes them, if nothing else, tight of frame, or so impossibly out of your league that you're attracted to the concept as much as the girl herself. For example, I use to beat it to Olivia Newton-John. That's right, I got physical Sandra Dee style on more than one occasion. Part of the attraction was her accent and smoking hotness. But a big part was that I was pretty sure that she wasn't going to swing by PS 121 to help out with my hand jive. It was the mystery that kept things exciting.

These days, I think people give away too much too soon. We treat sex like racquetball, slamming our bits about after a nonexistent warm-up only to change partners before we ever really get a grip on the game. The result? Twelve-year-olds are giving blowjobs on the bleachers while their parents dutifully sit through couple's counseling so they can move on to the next contestant guilt-free. Maybe I'm getting older, but this seems a little sad.

There's something to be said for delayed gratification. Whether it is waiting for a reasonable age for your first time or injecting romance and foreplay into an established relationship, the slow burn bakes best.

BAD ADVICE

Personal Finance
*****

"I can't believe what a bunch of nerds we are. We're looking up money laundering in a dictionary."
— Ron Livingston as Peter Gibbons in *Office Space*

*****

The only people who assert that money doesn't matter are those so far to either end of the fiscal spectrum that they've lost all perspective on reality.

Being poor sucks. There is no dancing around that fact. Sure, you can live on love and the occasional dumpster dive if you're a teenage poet backpacking his way through Europe. The sights and questionable sexual exploits are likely worth a bout of botulism and the occasional scrotum sore. But stretch the lifestyle into your late twenties and you quickly go from soul-searching artist to homeless vagrant. Trust me, college girls rarely blow the latter. Sooner or later, you'll realize that money matters and chicks actually dig guys with a place to live and the ability to spring for something more appealing than a double serving of ramen noodles. I'm not sure when it happens, but somewhere along the line, health insurance and a 401K become sexier than six-pack abs and the ability to burp the alphabet.

Of course, the super-rich are no saner. These freaks also claim that money isn't important, but that's only because they have so much that the simple concept of value has been distorted beyond recognition. Ask anyone with an annual combined family income of over 250k the price of a loaf of bread, and I guarantee they wouldn't have a clue. How the hell can you run a company, much less a country, if you can't balance a checkbook and think paying $7,000 for a handbag is a reasonable idea?

Yeah, I'm convinced that most people are fiscally retarded. But *you* don't have to be. Heed my advice, and your accounts and mental status will be better balanced.

I'm trying to sell my house. Should I hire a "staging consultant?"

I'm going to go with, "Are you shitting me?" as a response. What the hell are you expecting the buyer to say? Something like, "You know, I was in the market for a five-bedroom on the lake with a heated pool, but I have to say your feng shui approach to this trailer's outhouse really moved me on an emotional level..."

Seriously, I once had a real estate agent claim that a buyer backed out because the aura of my entryway wasn't inviting enough. I know it's a tough market, but I can only cater to crazy so much. Do yourself a favor: shitcan the guru and offer some cash to close. Greenbacks do amazing things for people's thought processes.

Is money truly the root of all evil?

No. Money is awesome. I highly recommend getting as much of it as you can. Blaming money for evil is like blaming a certain style of

BAD ADVICE

moustache for the extermination of six million Jews.

Freakin' poor people and their propaganda. It's insane. It's like those guys with the little dicks who swear that size doesn't matter. Trust me. I've been to prison. It matters.

- **A Related Note:** Okay, so perhaps the Jewish comment was over the top, but I was searching for a metaphor, or was that a simile? Christ (oops, I did it again). I'm like the dumbest writer on the planet.

Why do I have to pay school tax if I don't have kids? Can I get around it?

I wish, but it seems like the childless among us got the ass end of this little social contract. According to a recent county property tax statement seventy-two percent of the money goes to schools and five percent goes to "sheriff." (Seriously, *sheriff*?)

Anyway, this leaves me with two questions: Why are kids so stupid? And why are cops so prolific? With these investment figures, I should have a flying car invented by a preteen that easily evades the outdated radar technology of the donut dippers. Instead, I'm collecting tickets while pouring money into techno-dependent toddlers who can't put down their smartphones long enough to complete a coherent thought.

I realize "these kids today" have the attention span of a java-jolted spider monkey, but maybe that's because we've replaced books with gadgets and creative thought with Apple apps. If the Morrisville, North Carolina version of Rosco P. Coltrane can get the job done with a fleet-priced hemi and a little legwork, then precious little

JACKSON HOLIDAY

Susie should make do with a library card and some focus.

So I say, let's rethink our youth investment strategy, or at least turn their fleeting attention to pothole maintenance. If I'm going to be forced to fund the marginally effective education of other people's offspring, I should at least have some say in the curriculum.

I want to lease a luxury car, but it's a bit beyond my budget. Should I go for it?

Um, have you heard of this little thing called the recession? Want happiness? Live below your means, my friend. Don't be in such a rush to join the business Borg who latch on to what others do just because a critical mass thinks it's a good idea. I'm not in the habit of echoing liberal, political eggheads, but in this case I agree with Clive Hamilton, who said, "People buy things they don't need, with money they don't have, to impress people they don't like."

If you really want a fancy car, at least wait until you can afford it, and that means having the cash. Leasing a vehicle is like marching down to the county lock-up, dropping your drawers, and offering all takers a bang-one-get-one-free coupon.

No one likes being financially ravaged, but to me when the average Joe leases a Benz, a little James Dean in us dies.

BAD ADVICE

Sometimes I feel that successful people come from another planet. It's like they have something I don't. Is there any way to be more like them?

I've known a few amazing people and one thing is for shit sure — they don't whine. Building anything — a business, a relationship, or a foundation of knowledge — takes work, not words. Successful people, well, most anyway, are doers. There are talkers of course, but eventually someone calls their bluff.

- **A Related Note:** Great people are comprised not from a simple summation of all their positive attributes, but rather from the aura with which they surround themselves. Only they know exactly what makes up the aura, but I'm starting to believe it's a combination of unbridled self-confidence and the nurturing humility that comes from never forgetting whence you came.

I have a life coaching practice, but I feel bad about charging people. Why?

You do see the irony here, right? Coming to me for life coaching is like asking Genghis Khan about the salad fork.

You feel bad because, let's face it...life coaching is sort of a bullshit thing.

Just to be clear. No one makes money. They just take it away from other people. The business folk can yap all they want about customer focus and partnership, but in the end transactions are transactional and the sting you feel is a Visa-card-sized paper cut on your soul.

JACKSON HOLIDAY

I make lots of money, but the rest of my life is in the shitter. How can I be so successful in one area and such a failure in the others?

It's all about focus.

When I first achieved success, I found myself sitting alone in my great new house, paid for by my great new job, looking out the window at my great new car. It was nice for a moment or two, but as the day dragged on, I noticed how quiet it became and I started worrying about my health, my family and my love life...the things I had neglected in order to sit in that spot and the only things money couldn't provide.

Sounds like you've had a similar wake-up call. My advice? Try not to hit the snooze button.

I feel like customer service is going down the tubes. I got dissed at department store recently. Should I take my business elsewhere?

My standing rule is that no one out-jerks me. Wait, I just got that. Still, it's pretty true on both counts. Seriously, I have the forearms of Popeye the Sailor Man.

The other day the Lowes' guy took so long trying to locate the price for an item that while he was dick monkeying in the back room I ordered it online from the Home Depot and even negotiated free shipping. When he finally returned with a bucket of nothing and a boatload of excuses, I showed him the e-receipt and left.

When you make nothing, customer service is king. So chop-chop, biotch.

BAD ADVICE

How much should I save?

Experts say that it depends on your age, obligations and retirement goals. All true. For me, however, it comes down to having "fuck you" money. It's a simple formula, really. You calculate how much you need to walk away from your commitments for one year. Once you've amassed that much, you think about how much it would take to walk away forever. Then start saving.

Most people will never hit step two. Heck, even a year in the bank is a stretch these days. But it's a nice big-picture goal with some emotion behind it. Sure, we can all fantasize about the mansion and the yacht, but who has that frame of reference? Having the financial wherewithal to tell your boss to go shit in his hat is something we can all relate to.

Yes, this may seem harsh, but there is something liberating about having a ripcord. It means no one can mess with you. Oddly enough, having the ability to drop out actually reduces the likelihood that you will. It's like the burn victims who take less morphine when they are in control of the dispensing device.

Money gives you the option of owning your time, and in the end that's all you have. So save your cash and spend your moments…wisely.

My colleague is always ready to come out for drinks and happily accepts a free one. The thing is, he never buys a round. What gives?

I once had a coworker like that. He was so cheap that if you lent him a nickel, he'd squeeze the balls off the buffalo. It pissed me off, 'cause he was higher up the food chain and clearly made more money than I did.

JACKSON HOLIDAY

A group of guys were heading out for drinks and planned to confront him in the most embarrassing way possible. (What can I say? My friends are dicks too.) The thing is, he never showed. Turns out the special needs son he was supporting — on his own — died suddenly.

The point is, you never know what shit people are going through. Don't get taken advantage of, but don't be so concerned with who flips the check that you chase away everyone without an expense account.

This recession is a killer. Will the free market fix everything?

I know nothing of global financial policy and its relation to the economic climate. What I do know is that the term "free market" is derived from an actual street market in Europe where trained monkeys would groom the lice from patron's heads for free.

While we still have a host of monkeys loitering about our commercial infrastructure, two things have changed. First, nothing is free. And now, instead of fostering a mutually beneficial, customer-friendly atmosphere, the monkeys shit in your hat and then rob you blind.

What is the worst debt to have?

Never borrow anything from Satan or your mother-in-law. That said, credit cards run a close third. I recently asked the company (that I've been with for twenty years, mind you) what my monthly rate would be if I were to ever carry a balance.

She said, "The low-low interest rate of 20.99%."

"Are you shitting me?" I asked. "The Mafia doesn't have the balls to charge that much. It's no wonder people can't get out of debt. I'd honestly be better off with a loan shark."

There was a slight crackle on the line, followed by some nifty jazz. After a few moments, a supervisor came on the line, happy to report that because of my healthy credit score and years of patronage, my rate had been reduced to the "ultra low-low rate" of 18.99%.

I declared the change an outrage, citing my shock that he would dare adjust my account terms without my knowledge. I then demanded the original higher rate. He tried his hand at logic, but I spouted a variety of legal infractions and pressed the point. Apparently, I also pressed a nerve, because he actually cursed at me and hung up.

A few moments later, the phone rang. It was a senior supervisor with talk of an elusive, "super ultra low-low rate" of 17.99%. I walked him though twenty minutes of balance transfers, selected a new reward system, switched my card design and then canceled the sucker. I said it before. No one out-dicks me.

Is Black Friday shopping worth the hassle?

Depends on you what you value. I, for example, value my sanity and my freedom. Based on how I feel about most of humanity, if I ever went shopping the day after Thanksgiving I would likely fly into a murderous rage and let loose a wealth of carnage not seen since the Old Testament. And you know there were some bloodthirsty fuckers in that book.

JACKSON HOLIDAY

Such actions, of course, would either get me shot or, with my luck, shot, but not fatally and then life in jail. The thought of prison rape is bad enough. The idea that my story would likely be made into a *Lifetime* movie and that the resulting stardom would only increase said raping is worse. I'm no economist, but paying retail at a retail outlet seems the safer way to go for all concerned.

On a recent flight, I saw a roach in my overhead bin. Can I take legal action?

Unfortunately, in this country you can sue a mirror for giving you body image issues. I'm no Denny Crane, but while it may be within your rights, it seems like a pretty petty thing with which to clog up the legal system. After all, cockroaches have been flying for years. Just ask a Floridian. They call the cantankerous creatures palmetto bugs. They're nearly the size of a Cessna and are often inclined to use your head as a landing strip.

It's an unpleasant hassle, I admit, and perhaps one worthy of an upgrade, lounge card or stewardess-sponsored happy-ending massage in the lavatory. But compared to the magnitude of other corporate fuckery, I doubt your ambulance chaser will walk with a verdict on gross negligence. Grossness, maybe, but that just leads us back to the lavatory, now doesn't it? Actually, given the age, size and general demeanor of your average American flight attendant, I'd opt for the upgrade.

But seriously ...

The *Greed Is Good* gang will swear that life is a never-ending ascent. Winners reach for the sky,

BAD ADVICE

so if you're not building the empire, it's being torn down. Fair enough, I guess, assuming you're constructing something real. Of course, money is never truly made. It's exchanged. So perhaps the best you can do is have a little something up your sleeve to help with the slight of hand. Your pocket to mine, or so goes the mantra.

The Occupy crowd will chant that collecting coinage is akin to constructing a house of cards. Accounts can seem sturdy, but most are a breeze away from toppling. We've seen this to be true as well. But spreading wealth like peanut butter doesn't help either. You may end up with a stronger foundation, but you haven't built a freakin' thing. Congratulations, hippies, you strived for the ground floor and came up short.

No, money is a simple matter, with easy-to-follow rules. First, work your ass off to earn what you can. Second, live below your means. Finally, save for tomorrow, but realize it may not be scheduled. So splurge now and then on the little things that have big meaning.

Of course money isn't everything, so remember to invest in moments and in people. They pay dividends in memories and friendship. Both are sounder than stocks and real estate... always have been.

Other Random Nonsense
*****

"That opportunity could really open up a lot of windows for you."
– My sister-in-law, God love her.

*****

I'm lazy. We've established that. So once again I needed a catchall. It's not my fault, really. These were among the more intelligent questions I received. Seriously, writing this book has done wonders for my self-esteem. I may be a flatulent, illiterate lactard with an askew and altogether unimpressive penis, but at least I have a clue. Apparently, many of my readers would have a hard time finding their asshole with both hands and a funnel. But fear not, my sheep, your shepherd is about to lay the knowledge down up in here.

How do I make a Turducken?

You don't. There is nothing remotely appetizing about culinarily rapping a pre-sodomized piece of poultry. And going for a "beer-battered" approach is only making matters worse. Why not just date rape a Kentucky Fried six-piece and be done with it.

Look, you roofie-toting Iron Chef wannabe. Quit getting your recipe recommendations from Skeeter and the boys over at the county fair.

BAD ADVICE

Can you explain the structure of the universe?

Ummm, okay.

In the beginning, before the mass proliferation of aerobic workout videos and vitamin-infused water, the universe was embarrassingly fat and out of shape. It consisted largely of photons and bozons (mostly bozons). But there was one futon, and that, my friends, was a ridiculous substitute for a bed.

Why did the chicken cross the road?

I should stab you for asking, but instead I'll volley it back.

Do you actually care? We've hassled the poor bastard for years, as if knowing the answer would really solve anything. Try this: He crossed the road to see his lesbian, intravenous-drug-using aunt who was buying a three-legged poodle from a man named Argyle.

Well, there you have it. Any big revelations? Did that help you work through nuclear fusion? Chickens live for nothing and are basically the tasty cousin of the disease-infested pigeon. It's all very bleak, as I'm sure is your social life.

Any tricks for getting chips to fall from the vending machine when they get stuck?

It's moments like this when I realize I am writing for truly the lowest common denominator of literate humans.

No, my friend, beyond kicking, bitching and forking over another fistful of change, I can't help you. But I think your issue is more about seeking reassurance. And as you know, since it's better to give than receive (except when it comes to blow

JACKSON HOLIDAY

jobs), I think you should transfer this college angst into a helpful tidbit of information for your classmates.

Locate the closest functional vending machine and tape to it the following note.

THIS MACHINE IS IN ORDER

Granted, you may have just lost your entire life's savings on a women's field hockey game; the love of your life may have left you for a married, forty-two-year-old, out-of-work, jazz musician and your transitional lover may have begun to say things like, "Thanks, but I'd rather shop for dental floss." Still, this machine continues to work.

You see, amid all this chaos, all that is wrong with your life and mine, the miserable job, the forgotten dreams, the strange feeling you get when time passes and you realize you've just purchased a fresh vegetable of your own accord, this machine is happily humming along, quite secure in its future and role in society.

It's in order, in harmony, in that blissful nirvana some of us never find. But don't despair. You're just a couple of quarters away from an ice-cold Diet Pepsi, and that's a start.

I cry when I see those Tori Amos animal commercials. Is there something wrong with me?

Umm, are you raping dogs? Tori Amos is the sexual assault chick. The fembot you're thinking of is Sarah McLachlan. Get it straight and stop being a pansy. If you have to think of musically inclined liberal hotties think of them as lesbians

BAD ADVICE

in a poorly written porno where they reward you with an erotic threesome for saving their pet kitty. Yum.

If you could change one thing, what would it be?

That is a wise and slightly depressing question. We all dream of owning a time machine, a magical device that will let us go back just long enough to fight the bully, kiss the girl or say or unsay something life altering.

For me, the moment is pretty clear. I know the place, the time, and the person. The girl, really... it's always a girl, isn't it? Still, there are no time machines, and so I'll plead the fifth.

Any insight on the distribution logistics behind Easter?

I've struggled with this one for a while. I mean, Santa's got a sleigh, some flying reindeer...that makes sense. But the bunny is just a rabbit, right? How is he rocking the same productivity metrics...UPS? Outsourcing? A magical GTO? It's all very confusing.

- **A Related Note:** Christians get really pissed when you refer to Easter as "Zombie Jesus Day". They get even more annoyed when you causally hum Michael Jackson's "Thriller" with a twisted smile on your face.

What's up?

You know. Same shit. Different foot.

Do you like horror movies?

No. They are just too cheesy. For me, a horror film would be two minutes long.

"Dude," says random soon-to-be-killed extra, "I just saw a guy with a chainsaw and a ski mask go down that dark alley. I'm gonna check it out."

"Good luck with that," says snarky, handsome leading man (me). "I'm going to pop over to the pub for a pint and, you know, not die."

ROLL CREDITS

What's the best online email program?

You're shitting me. The closest thing I get to the web are the cobwebs on my condoms. I pick my email account based on Darwinian principles. Gmail just sounds gangster. I'm totally convinced that Gmail would shank Yahoo Mail in the shower if they did time together.

When will we get a flying car?

Never. First of all, our best minds are preoccupied with inventing the next version of Angry Birds. But even if we could invent a flying car, the government would never allow it to come to market. Have you been on the highways recently? I barely trust my fellow humans to stay on their side of a double yellow line. There's no way I'm leaving the house if these fuck nuts are given access to pitch and yaw controls.

- **A Related Note:** If cars were as reliable and efficient as toilets, they would run on water, clear waste instead of producing it, and require little more than a jiggle as a maintenance plan.

Is there any point to voting?

It depends. Are we talking presidential elections or wet T-shirt contests? In the case of the latter, of *course* there is. Just be sure to

BAD ADVICE

throw your support in an obvious way to the dark horse in the race. Chances are she won't win, but even if she's not the pick of the litter, in my experience, girls with big boobs and low self-esteem are appreciative of flattery. Play your cards right and you can Jedi mind-trick your way into an evening of motor-boating the bodacious tatas of some porn-extra wannabe you would have otherwise lacked the courage to approach.

On the off chance you meant an actual political contest, forget it. The Electoral College has been collectively casting the wool over our eyes since its inception. Sure it made sense in the Dark Ages, when Farmer Joe's rights were being trampled by the slick city folk of Philadelphia. But now? If you're a Republican in New York or Democrat in Texas and under the illusion that your opinion counts, check yourself into a mental institution. Call me cynical, but until my vote is actually counted, it doesn't freaking count.

Playing a game of telephone with your political opinions is like hiring an illiterate interpreter, employing a priest as theological middleman or jerking off into a tube sock.

What's harder — to "break it down" or to "keep it real"?

Put the book down and go flog yourself with a hot wire hanger. Seriously, right now.

- **A Reluctant Related Note**: I managed to break it down once. The thing is that when I tried to put it back together I ended up with three spare parts and a little less duct tape.

JACKSON HOLIDAY

How much should I spend each month on personal grooming?

Okay, this whole metro sexual thing has to end. Guys, good grooming is important, but when it gets to the point where you are creating spreadsheets to account for your pedicure purchases, you've gone too far.

The saddest part is that after college the average person spends far more on the outside of their head than they do on the inside. Gargle, clip your nails and shower on a regular basis. Then head over to Barnes & Noble and buy a book, preferably without sports stats or cartoons.

- **A Related Note**: You're a homo.

What's one "old school" thing that you miss?

Who you calling old school? Fine, you pre-pubescent techno-tard. I happen to miss the thoughtfulness of the phone booth. There's simply no app for shielding oneself from the rain or changing into Superman.

How do you cure a hangover?

What I do is have three or four cheese sandwiches and a Diet Shasta right before bed. The Shasta is the key, on account of the fizzies. Of course, I'm lactose intolerant and so the cheese makes me fart like a sick goose, but playing turtle with the girlfriend really distracts me from the spinning room and my pounding headache.

What's bothering you right now?

My balls itch. Want to lend a hand? I'm sure you're wearing one of those Star Trek earphones, so it should be a cinch.

BAD ADVICE

My friend uses foul language often, even though he knows it offends me. What should I do?

Shut the fuck up.

Sorry, couldn't resist. Seriously, sit the guy down, explain your point of view and ask that he clean it up where appropriate. Chances are he won't go Mormon overnight, but friendship is about balance. If he cleans it up around the office and family functions, you should forgive a little colorful vocabulary at the bar and occasional sporting event.

If he refuses to bend at all, get a new friend. No one likes an inflexible asshole.

Does violence solve anything?

Depends on how hard you hit.

In a perfect world, you could reason your way out of any situation. The ample application of empathy, facts and wisdom would defuse every altercation, from the schoolyard bruiser to the Middle-Eastern conflict. The unfortunate reality, however, is that people aren't too bright. It's not completely our fault. After all, assuming you believe in evolution, we're not that far removed from the fight-or-flight default setting of our shit-tossing ancestors. In the end, bullies exist.

It's actually an important question, and one I was forced to confront while operating a neighborhood martial arts school years ago. A religious woman, concerned with her son's potential participation, approached me with an earnest but accusatory question.

"How can you teach children to beat each other up?" she asked abruptly.

JACKSON HOLIDAY

"That's not what I do."

"I've seen you. My son sneaks out of swimming to watch your class. I caught him looking on just last week as you did some sort of an arm break. What kind of person shows little boys how to break arms?"

I sidestepped her question and countered with my own. "You're talking about the little blond kid, right?"

"Yes."

"He's been watching for a while now. What is he, about eight?"

"Seven."

"I see. Why do you suppose he's so interested in the class?"

"I know exactly why. Same as all the others. They want to fight. They want to punch each other and break arms and —" Her voice faded as she looked away.

"You think that's the only reason?"

"They're boys, aren't they? Boys love the rough stuff."

"I see," I said, with detectable uncertainty.

"You disagree?"

"No. No. It's just that we've been getting ready for a kata tournament and haven't really fought in a while. I doubt your boy...what's his name?"

"Jason. Jason Luke."

"...I doubt Jason has ever even seen the class spar."

"So?"

"Well, it just makes me think something else is pushing him to watch. Any idea what that could be?"

She drifted into thought for a moment, then returned with a sigh. "School. He's having problems with kids at school."

I offered a reassuring smile. "About half the students who come through that door are running from some wild-eyed bully. One chased *me* here years ago."

"Then you know what I mean. You know exactly why they want to learn."

"Sure, mass movie-like destruction; quick kills filled with blood and gore. But that's not what I teach them."

"Come on now. Don't you show them how to fight, how to stand up to people?"

"Absolutely."

"See, I can't compete with that. How can I raise my son to be a good Christian? How can I teach him about turning the other cheek if you're showing him how to bash it in? Religion is important in my family. I love my son and hate seeing him teased at school, but how can I send him to someone like you if what you teach goes against all I believe?"

Normally I'd offer some sarcastic retort, but I realized suddenly that the woman before me was actually a caring, competent mother. She wanted to do the right thing by her faith and her son without betraying either.

"Mrs. Luke, how easy do you think it is for Jason to run from the bullies?"

"I don't know. Not very, I guess."

"Really? I disagree. I mean if you had the choice between being beaten up or handing over your lunch money, wouldn't you 'turn the other cheek' and walk away?"

"Of course."

"But would you be doing so because it was something you truly believed in, or because you were scared of standing up?"

She opened her mouth quickly as if to answer, but nothing came.

"Mrs. Luke, I teach my students to travel to the heart of their fears. I push them and challenge them and train them until there is not a bully in the world they wouldn't fight if the need arose. Mrs. Luke, I'm not a Christian, but I understand the ideals. And I know without a doubt that when I choose to turn the other cheek to an aggressor it's because I *want* to, not because I *have* to. Under those conditions, doing right seems all the more real."

Two weeks later I received my student rosters for the following session. I wasn't too surprised to find Jason's name in my beginners class. I knew he'd weasel himself in sooner or later. It was the adult list that shocked me. I smiled when I read the name Marion Luke.

All snark aside, the only thing less effective than violence is cowardice. Call me crazy, but kindness and compassion seem to mean more when wielded by the mighty. The weak — well, their motives can always be called into question.

How do you know when you're officially an adult?

Some say graduation. For others, it's the first job or wife or kid. For me, it's when you stop asking for permission or approval. I can't picture my pop posing this question. So my guess is, if you're asking, you haven't hit the mark just yet.

But don't worry about it too much. From what I've seen, adulthood is overrated.

BAD ADVICE

Should I buy a Hummer?

Technically, I can't endorse prostitution, but....

Oh wait, you meant the vehicle. Well, my first inclination was to give you a literary bitch-slapping due to the sheer economic stupidity, but it might not be such a bad idea. Actually, the H3 is roughly the size of a Fiat. So what's the point?

I think the whole car industry is going bat shit. Hummers are getting smaller. Minis are getting bigger. When they meet in the middle like some automotive Benjamin Button, I think the universe may implode. That, or we will see the return of the wood-paneled station wagon. Either way, it's bad news.

Unless you are on active duty, forget the original Hummer. They just announce to the world that you have a small penis. Yup, I ended on a military-themed dick joke. Don't ask, but tell all your friends. Really. Book royalties rule.

But seriously ...

That's all I can bear in the way of random nonsense. Really, people, I feel dumber for having read your correspondence. I'm legitimately frightened and honestly concerned for your well-being. You should be ashamed of yourselves.

Still, you pay the bills and for that I adore you. And so I offer a few parting words of advice. First, don't breed. Based on your questions, no good can come from it. Second, try not to run with scissors unless you've recently updated your will citing me as beneficiary. Then by all means, scamper away. Finally, savor your moments. They are, by all accounts, too few and too fleeting. So smile, you fuckers. Life is a laugh.

Epilogue

Someone once said, "I don't enjoy writing. I enjoy having written." I researched the quote, pretty sure I wasn't the one who had uttered the statement. What I found surprised me. Lots of people plant a flag on the saying.

Laying claim to another's work is not uncommon...a simple hazard of the business, or so I'm told. But in this case, I suspect it was more misstep than malice: an honest error born from a blog-sponsored game of telephone and a simple affinity for the idea. The saying resonates, and that, give it wings.

I heard it first from Jack Klugman as Oscar Madison in *The Odd Couple*. Though I was only eight years old, the line stuck with me as if somehow foreshadowing a critical adult endeavor.

It's funny how words can do a number on you. So be mindful of what you read, what you say, and what you write.

It's true, of course. Writing *is* a painful process. And while most of us enjoy the end more than the start, beginnings hold the promise of a new adventure. In truth, the travel is what we crave.

Richard Bach once said, "Everything in this book may be wrong." Given the title of this work, a stronger sentiment may be warranted. Still, advice is free, and so it's up to you to decide what you carry away. I hope you collected a chuckle or two. That's the reason I start and the ending I strive for.